GOD OF A SECOND CHANCE

How to move on from your past and prepare for the next phase of your life by connecting with God

Compiled By

Best Selling Author

SHIRLEY D. LATOUR

Foreword by:
Kerry-Ann Zamore Frazier

SL
Elite Publishing

Special discounts for any *God of a Second Chance* or *Grace To Recover* Books are available on bulk quantity purchases by book clubs, churches, associations, support groups and other special interest groups.

Visit slelitepublishing.com

For details, email: support@slelitepublishing.com
Or call (254) 300-6027.

Keep searching back on Amazon.com for the release of the Audiobook on Amazon coming SOON!

DEDICATION

It is to You Lord I owe this honor. You have done it again, even through the many adversities set before many of the authors in this anthology. You shined Your light on us and helped us deliver the message to people everywhere so they too can have another opportunity, a second chance!

This book is dedicated to YOU, the many women and men who will brave the pages of this anthology to find a glimmer of hope in your situation. You may have thought it was over and there can never be another chance to get it right or recover from the mishap. Well sir or ma'am, think again! It is to you, the one who gave up on yourself because of a loss. Well it is NOT over, God is right there waiting for you! It is written that you may know you are NOT alone. God is not just a God of a second chance but as many as you need.

Be encouraged as you venture through every word!

CONTENTS

ACKNOWLEDGMENTS

To: DEMETRIUS GORDON, YVONNE TIJERINA, TORRI EUGENE, MONICA LATRICE WASHINGTON, WANDA "SISTAH SOLDIER" PETTY, HEIDI R. LOPEZ, DORLEAN WASHINGTON, MICHELE GRAHAM, AND SHANTA GREEN:

Without you being led of God to share your innermost truths with the world, this anthology would not be what it is: MARVELOUS, EYE OPENING AND INSIGHTFUL! Thank you for your willingness to be transparent and allow others to learn about you so that they too may know that God IS a Way maker, Promise Keeper, and Light in the darkness. Thank you for your heartfelt love, support and PATIENCE with me as your publisher.

To: Mrs. Shonda Curb, EXTRAORDINARY Woman of God and my main editor, THANK YOU for all your hard work on this project and the Grace To Recover series! You are truly a Godsend.

To: Mrs. Kerry-Ann Zamore Frazier, the one and ONLY, best Playwright, Screenplay, filmmaker this side of heaven, mom, wife, businesswoman, community advocate and so much more: THANK YOU for taking time from your non-stop schedule to read the book in its entirety and write the foreword.

Travon and Welina, my reasons for breathing and pressing forward in life: this is my gift to you and I pray someday you will cherish what you have been given. I love you both always! Go do GREAT THINGS according to what God has placed in YOU!

FOREWORD

God of a Second Chance is an outstanding masterpiece spearheaded by the visionary Shirley D. LaTour. This survey of personal stories, expounds on the overwhelming conception that God is a friend, a lover, a confidant, a Redeemer, a Savior, and a God of a second, third, tenth and twenty-first chance. It is a reminder, that God's love, mercy and grace, is astounding to those who hear and listen to his voice and He truly shows how He is able to comfort and restore in these inspiring revelations.

Shirley LaTour has truly brought a group of dynamic community leaders together to write a series of compelling and inspiring stories from which anyone who is willing to listen and gain understanding will truly be impacted to live beyond a life of destitution, depression, complacency and lack. From the Dedication penned by LaTour herself; "It is to You Lord I owe this honor. You have done it again, even through the many adversities set before many of the authors in this anthology. You shined Your light on us and helped us deliver the message to people everywhere so they too can have another opportunity, a second chance" to, the final words of Overcomer Shanta Green; "No matter what we may endure in life we must find the strength to keep going. Everyday we are given a second chance at life. I plan on living each day to the best of my ability, not taking anything or anyone for granted", this book is a challenge to trust that God has the ability to make all things new.

I read each line, with tears streaming down my cheeks, as I too received the revelation that God is truly a friend, and the Almighty, who is able to give us a second chance through his grace. This engaging book is a continuation of Grace to Recover, LaTour's first book, it expresses the steps of how to truly live an abundantly flourishing life knowing that God has given the opportunity for us all to start over no matter where we are in life, no matter what mistakes have been made. This book relates to all, no matter the socio-economic, racial identity or religious preference, it is truly a book that bespeaks of healing and restoration of the soul.

Kerry-Ann Zamore Frazier LCSW, MSED, Minister

INTRODUCTION

Have you ever thought, "I messed up my life." "There will never be another chance at love and marriage, happiness, job or life opportunities." "I've done wrong so my children were taken and I'll never get another chance to parent well." "I'm being punished by God" "I'm worthless so it does not matter how I treat my body" etc. We've all said something to that effort and felt sorry for ourselves, if but for a moment.

This anthology's writers will certainly give you a different perspective, a new way of looking at life after forging through the backdrop of our lives. We have encountered:

1. Loss of marriages
2. Terrible circumstances due to loss of self
3. Life altering ordeals and tragedies such as loss of children or siblings, health
4. Mind-bending hang ups

YET we are alive today to show you just how great our God is at giving you not just a second chance, but as many chances as you need!

If you have it all together and don't need God to give you a second or the millionth chance, this book is NOT for you. But, if you are seeking truth and tips from ordinary people that chose to connect with God, their Lord and Savior and were brought out of captivity so they can impart to you, read on!

As the visionary author who brought these women together I can say with certainty these are the true stories we need in today's world. We need the hope that each story provides. I was touched and encouraged even as I was reading to start the editing process and get the stories in the order I thought they should go. I've encountered some life altering events as well but I have overcome, only by being connected to God, through Jesus, the one SOURCE.

In this book, *GOD OF A SECOND CHANCE,* you will learn how to forget the past and push forward to your future by: reaching for God and surrendering to Him, forgiving yourself and others and having faith to believe that second chances are truly possible.

There are hurting people everywhere around the globe. It does not matter where we come from. Tragedy strikes us all but you can know and understand today that the One and Only True Living God is there to pick you up and give you a second chance at life.

Authors in this anthology originate from West Africa, California, several cities in Texas, New York: some are Veteran Women, others are married to Service Members and others still have no military affiliation. As you see in the diversity here, we can assure you that no matter where you live there is someone going through the same thing. You are NOT alone.

The past is over and we can do life again. Read on to see how it is possible! We assure you that you will learn at least one thing to help you push to your future.

1

THE AUDACITY TO GET UP

Shirley D. LaTour

This is my SheStory

Curled up on her side of the California King-sized bed, tears flowing in silence as she mourned: the loss of love, the loss of her former cheerful self, the loss of innocence she felt had been snatched, the loss of HER.

Where oh where had she gone? Had she even given herself permission to see the light of day? Had she forgotten she was loved by Almighty God? The One who knew and loved her before she was ever conceived in her mother's womb?

She was broken and bruised. Married, yet lonely and in despair. Feelings of fear, sadness, inadequacy, frustration, depression and guilt overwhelmed her. She was caught in a trap; a trap that said she was nothing and nobody so why put up a fight?

Why should she pray? Why should she meditate on God's Word? Why should she even bother living? What was the use? Nothing she did seemed to make things better. The smile was all a facade to cover the pain in her eyes and heart.

Have YOU ever felt any of these feelings?

Costly Quietness

She allowed those close to her to walk over her, to cheat on her and to lie straight to her face. Though she knew the truth, she was paralyzed to act on the premonitions. Why? She felt worthless. She'd lost her self-esteem and was so unsure of whom to tell who'd even believe a word she uttered.

So she kept quiet, put up a cool front. It was better that way as long as she could function at work and get the children to school and extracurricular activities. No one had to know. Not the Pastor, oh, he was the one in violation. But she had faults too.

She gave away her power and allowed herself to lose focus on God. She used work and business as her coping mechanisms, not realizing she was not fully obeying God. Sound familiar anyone? It's okay, now you recognize it and can turn it around!

God had certainly been her Provider, her Source and Strength but she felt she could handle it without HIM. She had inadvertently and unknowingly placed a man above God and that was damaging. BUT GOD!

Pride had her believe if she just did it this way or that way, things would change. Her eyes were blinded, not accepting it as pride. She had no need to seek the One with every answer. She sought Him at times but surely came with complaining and blaming instead of coming humbly before the throne of grace.

She had her own issues not dealt with and was surely in need of God's redeeming grace, a second chance to do it His way. She needed to surrender her will to Almighty God and to seek Him while He may be found. Is 55:6

When she did this one thing, come humbly before Him, The One and Only True God, the Triune God stepped into her situation and DELIVERED like NO ONE else ever could! It's not that she'd done so well or been so good, it's because HE, the Lord of heaven and earth, is THAT GOOD! He is "God of A Second Chance".

Bringing It All Together

You may be wondering what in the world I'm referring to or getting at so allow me to lay the groundwork, the backdrop if you will.

The term "audacity" in dictionary.com is "boldness or daring, especially with confident or arrogant disregard for personal safety, conventional thought, or other restrictions." There came a time when I was married that I was going through so much warfare, it seemed unreal. I had to have the audacity, the boldness to take the necessary steps in the spirit to overcome the trials.

Curve balls, darts, arrows, downright bullets were being thrown and where coming from every which way. One early morning in late 2016, I was on a prayer call. The prophetess on the line, whom I did NOT know personally nor did she know of me, said something that made every hair on my body stand up.

She said something to this effect: Someone is going through in your marriage. You need to anoint your mattress with oil. You do not need to say anything to him. As he is sleeping, gently put your hand on him and pray to yourself.

With this, at first I will admit it scared me and I didn't necessarily WANT to put oil on my bed. Needless to say, my flesh wasn't all the way dead yet.

However, one day that week the mister came home on another tangent. I was tired of dealing with whatever was going on in his world that he refused to address and was taking out on me. There was a world wind in the house that night but the next day he was going out of town on temporary duty for a week.

What did I do, you ask? You got it. Not only did I anoint the mattress by sprinkling the oil that I'd prayed over on it, I SATURATED that mattress on his side, anointed every wood post, the headboard, etc.

I fasted and prayed every time he went out of town for a week at a time and anointed every surface of the house, especially our room, etc. I stopped fighting with carnal words or no words at all and began to speak the Word of God over every situation, over my mind and over everything that concerns me.

I was feeling so defeated and under condemnation for much of my life but God allowed me to go to a ministry that was preaching the unadulterated Word of God in November 2016. It seemed like every message was for me. Revelation knowledge hit me almost with every sentence and my Spirit man began to thrive again.

Can I tell you that you can be a believer, yet be bound by things, people, or circumstances? You can. For sure. Check out Luke 13:10-16. Eighteen (18) years worth of demonic forces over the life of this woman who was a believer and for me it was 16 years.

I didn't know I had the power in my tongue to change everything around me so God showed me I had it. I just needed to know how to use what He gave me!

You have that same power if you are a Believer! Jesus said, "I tell you the truth, anyone who believes in me will do the same works I have done, and even greater works, because I am going to be with the Father." John 14:12 NLT.

The key words are: anyone who believes in me (Jesus). You must first believe IT, whatever IT is, is possible, according to His Word and His will.

When Jesus left the earth in the natural, He left the Holy Spirit, The Comforter, our Leader and Guide to dwell in us. This is how and why we as Believers have the same power. It is His power on display but He works THROUGH us.

As my faith began to rise again, God moved obstacles out of my way. We don't have to climb the mountain as the once popular gospel song says. The Word tells us in Matthew 21:21 that if we have faith, we can SPEAK to the mountain and it will be cast into the sea.

See? Our words are POWERFUL! Remember though, not just the good things we speak will come to pass but the bad things too. Sometimes, even as believers, we curse ourselves due to the words we speak over ourselves and over our circumstances.

If you believe THE Word, not your word, have faith and don't doubt, it will be done. I had to start truly believing every Word of the Lord and speak it out of my mouth.

Your second chance will come around when you believe Him on the next level. Speak the Word over your life, your spouse's life, the lives of your children, your job: EVERYTHING THAT CONCERNS YOU.

On March 4, 2017 I went to see the movie *THE SHACK* and it catapulted me to the next level of trust in God. Here is how:

I had been fasting and praying diligently for a change to come since early 2016. I wanted my marriage to work but both spouses have to want it and take the necessary to make changes. I had released the guilt, shame and hurt of what was happening.

In August 2016, I started reaching out to other women as God instructed for me to do. All the while I did not know it was this that would ultimately set me free both in spirit and physically.

I had forgiven my husband for the things he was doing and just kept listening for the next instruction of the Lord. I took my eyes off him and placed them solely on God.

Things were breaking but slowly. Then I saw the movie (that my children wanted to see but I had paid no attention to on the TV commercials.) A scene came up that changed my perspective forever.

If you've ever seen *The Shack*, you will know what I'm talking about. The dad, Mack, who lost his five year-old daughter to a serial killer by way of rape, had been in a deep depression, struggling to understand. He had been judging the killer, his natural father and his heavenly Father for years.

He is put on the judgment seat, not to be judged but to be the judge of his two remaining teenage children. He is asked to make a decision of which of his children should go to heaven and which of the two should go to hell.

Of course Mack cannot decide and then has his breakthrough. He finally understands and allows God to be the judge of the killer and his father.

This scene erupted much emotion in me and brought me to my knees when I got home. I asked God to forgive me for judging my husband instead of lifting him up. I didn't realize I still had a spot of unforgiveness there.

That one spot had caused a delay in everything God desired to do. He waited on me to give it ALL to Him and allow Him to handle it His way. I yielded my will to His Will and He started moving even more on my behalf.

The end of the movie shows Mack being restored and his family being restored to the love they once knew before the tragedy. That second chance did not come until Mack surrendered everything and everyone, including himself, to God.

It was as if God made the movie for me in a deliberate span of time and used my children to get me there. The other movie I know was meant for me was *War Room*, released in August 2015…with these tools, the Word of God and an Apostle bringing life through the Word, I experienced signs, miracles and wonders in my life!

Only Through Obedience and a Surrendered Heart

One of the synonyms for audacity is the word "pluck". Google defines the term pluck as to "quickly or suddenly remove someone from a dangerous or unpleasant situation". I truly experienced a plucking right out of the hands of the enemy.

Once I gave TOTAL surrender to the One who had always been there and defended me, protected and shielded me, the enemy had no choice but to let go of me.

But I had to first have the audacity to get up: in mind, in heart, in deeds INDEED! I was not out willfully sinning; however, because my spirit man was wounded and I wasn't quite sure how to fight the battle I kept losing until...

Here is the scripture James 4:6-8 NLT that backs me up in this very saying:

And he gives grace generously. As the Scriptures say, "God opposes the proud but gives grace to the humble." **So humble yourselves before God. Resist the devil, and he will flee from you.**

In the King James Version, it says to submit to God. Well I was busy judging the wrongs of others towards me instead of presenting myself to God, holy and acceptable.

August 2017 was the culmination of much fasting and prayer that changed ME more than anyone else. It is when he came home with divorce papers, an agreement of what I wanted so that it could be filed.

It came when I didn't expect it, though the topic had come up many times. I was at PEACE, already prepared for what was next. I continued to treat him with respect throughout the difficulties and allowed God to do the work.

I didn't know which way it would go but I trusted God in the process. I knew He would take care of me regardless of how it went. HE HAS NEVER FAILED ME!

Today I stand in bold faith, knowing that NOTHING can by any means harm me. I am the head and not the tail. The lender and not the borrower. There is power in my tongue (so be careful what I allow to roll off of it).

I have been a single mom of a college son and teenage daughter since January 2018 and I have lacked NOTHING. Though my household income was cut by ¾, meaning out of four (4) pieces of the pie, I only get one (1) piece now and receive no child support.

God has truly supplied all my needs according to HIS riches in Glory. My son's college is COVERED (not out my pocket!), all my bills are paid, I still live in a spacious home and even got an upgraded car.

I tell you these things not to brag on me but on the God I serve! He made SURE everything was in place for me and that there was NO GAP in provision for my children and I.

I cannot say I am perfect. I am far from it but because I belong to HIM and hung in there according to His instructions, He DELIVERED ME.

Since the time of the divorce I can say I am truly happy and blessed beyond measure. I may not have all my desires but I KNOW HE watches over me.

My joy came back and my peace returned in the midst of the trial. I was no longer dependent on a man but my focus shifted to THE MAN!

Though I am a Registered Nurse by education, he SHIFT-ED my course and I'm so grateful. In obedience to His voice in the night October 2018, these books and my publishing company were birthed. To date three (3) books have been published in 2019.

I have a radio show that kicked off in February 2019 called "Prison Break: Breaking Down Walls Mind, Body and Spirit". It airs every Monday night from 6-7pm CST. I NEVER imagined ANY of this possible but God gave me a second chance to live FREE of the curse of condemnation and reclaim everything stolen from my life.

Opportunities come to me and not the other way around. I am not chasing the dollar; it is chasing me (just putting that in the atmosphere!)

There is no more sadness, depression, fear or anxiety in my life. That was all defeated on the cross: I allowed it to hang around for years but no longer.

With the divorce came freedom but I mean divorce in every sense of the word. I divorced fear and doubt. I divorced depression and everything associated with it.

I divorced judgmental spirits and religious beliefs. It was replaced with my relationship with God and agape love for others. It was there well before that point but it was hampered by unforgiveness.

A few examples of those who were given a second chance BECAUSE they chose to get up:

1. Abraham-though he stumbled and had a son outside the will of God trying to *help* God (thanks wife), God still allowed his promised son, Isaac, to be born in his old age. Remember he still had a choice to make. Genesis 21

2. King David-he committed adultery, murder, and had a child outside of covenant as a result of that adulterous relationship. Yes the first of their children died and King David mourned his loss even while he was still alive. However, he repented, got up and washed his face, then worshipped the Lord. He comforted his wife, made love to her and God blessed them with another son who was MIGHTY-Solomon. They were told to name the son Jedidiah, which means *loved by the Lord.* (sounds

like a second chance to me!) Read 2 Samuel chapters 11 and 12.

3. Rahab-she was a harlot but because she reverenced the men of God, the chosen people, she and her whole household was spared from death. Her descendants still live in Israel. See Joshua 6:25

As you can see, none of them did everything right or according to God's will at first but they were given a second chance. None of us are perfect. We have ALL done something that should've landed us killed, in jail or in a mental institution. But Jesus the Christ loves us so much and wants us to have a second chance with God.

It could be a second chance, a third or whatever number you are on. He is waiting on you to make the choice to get up.

You might say, "Well Lord I've done all you required of me. I haven't done any of the things THEY did and I've lived according to Your Will. Why me?"

Job is a prime example of someone who was upright before God yet he had to suffer the loss of everything so God could prove to the devil Job's stance in God.

Job proved his stance and was granted double for his trouble. So take heart and get up. Double is on the way.

I am learning of Him daily and marvel at all He has done in and through me. I just want to leave you with this:

Sister, brother, son, daughter, you CAN get up! No matter what you have faced in life, whether it was the loss of a loved one through death, divorce or simply a breakup; lost opportunity; lost identity; loss of health, self esteem or self worth; loss due to drug or alcohol addiction; loss of your family, loss of your finances, your home or ANYTHING else: I say to you, ARISE, GET UP.

"Talitha koum" which means "Little girl, get up!" in Mark 5:41 (NLT) are the very words of Jesus to a little girl who was literally dead in her bed. At that moment she got up off her deathbed and walked around.

You CAN GET UP! It is your choice. You are more than a conqueror through Christ who loves you Romans 8:37.

He gave me a second chance and I look forward to EV-ERYTHING He has in store for me.

Have the audacity to get up!

My prayer for you:

> Father I thank you for a second chance to
> serve you wholeheartedly.

I thank you for every person who reads these words that they are touched, healed and delivered of every curse of the enemy. I proclaim You are GOOD, The God of the universe and able to do exceedingly, abundantly above all we could ask, think or imagine! May their lived be changed from this day forward, relying on You for their every need and may they have the audacity to get up from a low place, trusting that You, Holy Spirit will lead and guide

God is so grand! He will allow your past to catapult you to your destiny...if you let Him! Are you in motion? Did you get up yet?

YOUR TAKE AWAYS FROM THIS CHAPTER

2

WHERE IS MY BOAZ?

Demetrius Gordon

The big "D." Divorce. How in the world did I end up here? Poor choices and not listening to my parents is my first answer. That's really the truth, but if I stop to think about it, it's a bit deeper than that.

I am and will always consider myself to be a PK. What's a PK? Preacher's kid. It wasn't as tough as some people think. Maybe because my parents didn't have us in church ALL THE TIME nor did we have mandatory family bible study. We went to church every Sunday and we also went for choir practice, and special occasions and functions.

Yeah, I know everyone thinks of PK's as being wild, but I know I didn't fit that stereotype. So, I wonder how many of us really were THAT wild. I guess enough of us to make the stereotype stick, huh?

Well, I wasn't wild like the stereotype, but I definitely had been raised to have a mind of my own so...I couldn't wait to breakout. Like most teenagers, I thought I was ready for the world. What I and most teenagers or young adults are really ready for is to break free of adult supervision. The limiting curfews and rules.

Adulting meant being able to do what I wanted and when I wanted. Of course, I didn't understand bills, traffic tickets, mortgages, etc. I also didn't understand that no matter where you go or what you do, there are a set of rules (laws) there for you to govern yourself.

I was still pretty naïve even though I thought I wasn't. So, when I ask myself, "How in the world did I end up here?" when I think deeper, the first thing that comes to mind is guilt. Yes, guilt. I was the good girl all through school.

With my Dad being an Army Chaplain, that meant we'd packed up about every 4 years and we would move to a different state or country, but the expectations were still the same. Remember who you are, whom you represent (God and family) and act accordingly.

I had no problems remembering that until I met him, the guy that would become my first husband; and, then I decided that SOME of our family principles and the Godly principles I had learned no longer applied to me. You know the ones that were no longer convenient for me to remember because I was in a "situation".

So I think it's an accurate description when I answer that question and say guilt and disappointment are what came to mind. And that's what breaking free of adult supervision felt like for me.

I grew up with my faith in God but got distracted so easily. It seemed like all the key things that I was taught just flew out of the window. It's a shame too because I could have saved myself a lot of trouble had I stuck to what I learned.

I was playing Russian roulette with my mind, body and soul. I had become sexually active after graduation, deciding that he was my "everything" and then one thing led to another. So…you guessed it.

I'm in my sophomore year in college and I'm pregnant and living with him. He had asked me to marry him before, but something wasn't right even outside the arguments, verbal and physical altercations. I couldn't put my finger on it. I couldn't see the forest for the trees.

Something had kept me from marrying him, but nothing could convince me to leave him so right before our baby turned one, I agreed to tie the knot. I thought I might as well marry him because clearly, I'm not going anywhere.

All I could hear in the back of my mind is, "I'm out here fornicating and having babies out of wedlock. Out here sinning and if I'm not going to leave him, we might as well get married." So, we got married. Jumped the broom. Tied the knot. I think you get the idea.

Anyway, I thought marrying him would make me happy because I wasn't shacking up with him; we were married so our child had a family and we were all under one roof. I also thought tying the knot would make him happy because I thought the main source of his unhappiness was that I wouldn't commit but it didn't mean a hill of beans.

Here I am doing things the "right way" now and wondering why things weren't changing for the better. It seemed that everything got worse. Our relationship was so tumultuous. We were already fighting, and he was accusing me of cheating and then he was hitting me.

For a while I didn't tell anyone because I felt like I deserved it. I wasn't the woman, wife, or parent I was supposed to be, so I thought. He did a real number on me to the point I felt like there wasn't any point in trying anymore and I contemplated suicide. But when I opened up to my Mom, she said things that I needed to remember about myself.

Mom's Sound Advice

1. I was not raised to be mistreated by anyone or anything on God's planet.

2. I had already been raised and no one else should be raising a hand to me.

3. I always had a home and that I was not forced to stay in my current situation.

4. If I chose to stay, I needed to remember to put God first and that He would point me in the direction that I needed to go.

5. She also reinforced that I was fiercely independent and that if things didn't work out that I was strong enough to stand on my own.

These were all the things I needed to hear to start the wheels turning in my head.

Because my Mom reminded me who I was and to whom I belonged, there came a point where I decided that things had gotten too bad; and, if I was going to do bad, I would do it all by myself.

Disappointment due to The Golden Example

I was also really disappointed because I got married thinking that it would last like my parents' marriage had. FOR-EVER.

But after two and a half (2-½) years our marriage was over and after almost four (4) years we were divorced. We tried talking. We tried not fighting. In the end, he wasn't willing to go to counseling and I wasn't willing to continue getting beaten up verbally or physically or to being held by gunpoint.

I had such a hard time deciding to let go of our marriage. I prayed, prayed, prayed, and prayed again. I kept looking at my parents who had been married for longer than I had been alive and just couldn't let go of what divorce meant to me. It meant so much. It meant that I didn't know how to fix my marriage, that I had made a bad decision, had failed, and then given up.

My parents' relationship wasn't rainbows and unicorns, but they made the relationship work. Through good and bad, the ups and downs, through everything. Why couldn't I do that? I'll tell you why I couldn't. Remember I prayed for an answer that would guide me and I received it.

I was in church one day and a gentleman in his 40s or 50s was giving a testimony. He was very nicely dressed. He looked like he smelled good. Seemed pretty well spoken. You know the kind of guy that we all say that we want. Well, he talked about how he and his wife had married young: how she had stuck with him through his partying and staying out all times of the night with him coming home drunk. Through his womanizing and not coming home, and through his general disrespect of her, their relationship and their home.

He was giving her praise for sticking with him through all of that and praying him through to be the man that she knew he could be. Sounds like an awesome testimony, right?

For some it might be but for me, it was what I needed to hear to let go of my marriage and move on. Here's why…what I heard was this woman was miserable for all the years her husband was mistreating her.

Remember they got married young and now I'm looking at a man in his late 40's, early 50's who says that he is finally the man that she knew he could be. I HEARD what he was saying, and it sounded so similar to what I was just starting to go through.

What? Oh, no! I decided right then and there in church that I didn't want to be miserable for two decades or more before I was happy. I would rather be miserable by myself than to go through all of that. I thought about the kind of mother I would be to our child, being constantly miserable. I reminisced about the example of disrespect we would be modeling for our child and what all of that would mean for their emotional wellbeing.

I told God that I heard him loud and clear. What I didn't realize then was that he wasn't for me and I wasn't for him. In other words, God didn't give him to me, nor did God give me to him so we were destined to struggle.

Thirteen years of not being married

So now I'd kissed my frog and he remained a frog. What's next? I prayed. Despite my mind being made up and feeling like it was the right decision, I still had a hard time with the fact that my marriage was on its last leg. I convinced him to get out of the military so I could go in. Because of my Dad's military service, I knew what I was getting into and I knew that there were a lot of essentials that I wouldn't have to worry about.

I knew the Army was the place for me. Not having to worry about having a roof over our heads, having food on our table, and having access to medical care meant a great deal of anxiety was erased. To top it off, I had the honor of serving our country while being in the medical field.

Now, we know how having an "ex" goes and I'm sure you can guess that it wasn't all peaches and cream. It definitely wasn't. I had constant reminders that I was still tied to my bad decision. They included, but are NOT all inclusive:

> His non payment of child support, return-
> ing our child almost two weeks after the new

school year started from being on summer break, blowing up my phone or showing up to my job trying to convince me to get back together.

He even told the court that I had abandoned our child while I was deployed to Iraq so that he could gain custody, and of course there was the second custody battle that started as soon as I got back to the States.

The first one was after he attempted to kidnap our child and take him off a federal installation. You would think those constant reminders would be enough for me to give up dating altogether, but nope. I kept trying. Now, of course, I would take time to myself. I would read self-help books, do new things, meet new people, go to bible study and church but I got lonely a lot.

In my mind I was not supposed to be alone, but with each ended relationship I was more and more disillusioned. And the cycle would repeat. I could still say that I wasn't nearly as miserable as I would have been had I remained in my first marriage.

My marriage today

Today, my second marriage is absolutely nothing like my first. It's so funny because I was at a point in my life where

I had just resigned myself to being single for the rest of my life, as in FOREVER. So, I didn't even see him coming.

We had friends in the same circle, so we had become familiar with each other. We worked together professionally on a few projects and were even on a bowling team together, so we became friends. He was so familiar that when he gave me a heads up about his pending divorce and asked me to help him celebrate it being final in a little more than a month, I thought he might be trying to hit on me but I dismissed it with a "naw…that's Gordon. He would have said something way before now".

You see? In the past, I had guys that had approached me with different variations of why they weren't with their spouse. You know, the "we're going through a divorce", or the "we're separated" and that they would like to "see" me. So my hubby's approach was very foreign to me.

His approach was so respectful and that in itself was such a wonderfully refreshing breath of fresh air. We respected each other personally and professionally; and, at times it felt like we were brother and sister from different parents, if that makes sense! We had both grown up with a keen sense of right and wrong, we were both fiercely loyal, and ridiculously silly. Everything just felt right!

Now of course once we decided to be in a relationship with each other things got a bit more interesting. We had more talks, heart to hearts, digging deeper into who we were. What was amazing was that we shared past hurts, joys, disappointments, and amazing experiences in our lives with each other and it never felt like judgment, just learning each other. And even though things felt different from previous relationships I still didn't trust it.

This old saying kept playing in the back of my mind, if it seems too good to be true it's because it is. I gave him the hardest time almost every step of the way because I didn't trust that he wouldn't do me the way every other person I had been in relationships with had done in the past. I had learned the hard way that different didn't always mean good.

He hung in there though, reassuring me each step of the way. Now, after combining our families and homes, we're getting ready to celebrate our 14th year wedding anniversary as of 2019! I love and respect the precious gift that God sent my way! And you know what? I ended up being happier, so much happier at least seven (7) years ahead of schedule!

Lesson Learned

I felt like I had lived a lifetime by the time I was 25. I learned some very valuable lessons about relationships and myself in general. Of course, there were some positives from my first marriage: our child and the fact that I learned a lot about myself during that time.

I learned to value myself and set the tone for how everyone treated me and to never accept disrespect in any form.

I learned what I was willing to put up with and the things I wasn't willing to compromise. I also learned to trust myself again, my gut, my discernment.

I would like to say that I've learned patience but God is definitely still working on me with that! But I can say that I have definitely learned to trust in God and know that his timing is always perfect.

And lastly, it might feel good but does it feel right? That was the question I asked myself in each relationship. That question and the power of prayer, I believe, are what kept me until my Boaz arrived.

YOUR TAKE AWAYS FROM THIS CHAPTER

45

3

RIDE OR DIE:
For Toxic or Freedom

Yvonne Tijerina

As I sit here recapping my 38 years of life what can I tell you about the paths I have chosen so far in my Journey that would intrigue you enough to reflect on your own choices? You may be taking your second chance for granted but I can testify that second chances do come abundantly! Sit back and reflect on things that may have been a second chance and you either did not realize it or just blew off.

Here is the truth of my personal acknowledgements. I did not start nor navigate to the end of each challenge alone. Each thought, word and step experienced, no matter what the situation looked like, was governed by ELOHIM.

Prayerful generations before me & seed bearers strategically placed in my path to give me knowledge or insight, finding good ground, sowed into me. Subconsciously, my ear to hear, my inner spirit that guards my seed of faith was listening for JEHOVAH'S guidance even before I understood that I knew the sweet sound of THE CREATOR'S voice.

Listen! Before you read any further, literally get your cell phone or grab your Bible and read *Mark 4:13 – 20*. The meaning is all the same so read it in whatever Bible version you like. You need to understand that no matter what your current issues or circumstances may look like right now or how they have looked like in the past, you are good ground. Your second chance to stand firm footed in your purpose starts with you accepting freedom.

"Freedom" {noun} - the power or right to act, speak, or think as one wants without hindrance or restraint. `` *Oxford Dictionaries © Oxford University Press, 2017.* In my experience and opinion, the transparent truth about your Freedom is simply this: Your circumstances are just a lock on a door, and you have always held ownership of the key that unlocks it.

The two things hindering you from unlocking it and walking through the door: 1. Your decision of how bad you want it or 2. The idea of what freedom means. For a time, I just liked the idea of what freedom meant but was unwilling to take the next step.

It did not matter that I was strong-willed with a Hell on Wheels temper and mouth, nor did it matter that my heart, with its own shields, though not impenetrable, hung on my sleeve. What mattered was that I had not yet had enough: enough of allowing others "guardianship authority" (Power of Attorney so to speak) to dictate my worth and how my worth was defined.

What I had to realize is that the vices that bind you and that may even be intergenerational, are truly escapable. You will need to realize this too. You must be willing to make decisions that will lead to your freedom. I was afraid of those decisions. Are you?

I was afraid of putting in twenty plus years of sharing life experiences with someone just to tear it down to the foundation and have to rebuild all over again. That would have been repeating the same mistakes of my parents and others whose influences were accepted in shaping the ideology of what my life should look like. I did not want to go through that. Nor did I want to deal with the disappointment, said and unsaid, that I felt and knew I would receive from my elders.

You see? I am the strong-willed child that listened, calculated consequences, and adhered to most of the rules. I am the oldest girl and I'm supposed to set a good example for those under me. So, for eight years of marriage, in moderate silence, I fought with and against my former spouse.

Why? Because I was too stubborn and scared to walk away from what had become toxic to me. I felt that enduring the relationship was what was right and expected of me. I was consumed with the opinions of others about my life. Even with them being unaware of all the venomous parts to my marriage with my ex-husband. I hid until I could not and did not want to hide the misery anymore. In year nine, I ignored the moral ideologies of my upbringing and I rebelled.

For the first time in my life I even whined like a damsel in distress for help, though my actions did not reflect that I wanted or needed help. Without realizing it, I had granted my ex-husband and those around me even more authority. Looking back, I can tell you that by rebelling I signed my own name as victim to those unseen guardianship authority papers. But all was not lost!

Awakening began with, "I will not be a victim anymore!" When you have been victimized in any way it is so easy to just play the role of a victim; to point fingers at those who hurt you and say, "Look what you did to me!" It is so easy to revert to silence. It is so easy to accept blame placed on you by the victimizer, by others or self-inflicted blame.

What matters is when you truly have had enough and want deliverance, NOT just to escape, because if you just escape you can be recaptured. You must want to be delivered.

My need for it outweighed my fear of it so, in the middle of my bedroom floor, on my knees with my belly flat on my thighs. My face to the floor, full of tears and snot. Pain radiating from my spirit through my flesh. I cried out to GOD!

Time stood still.

As I laid there, out of Man's concept of time, but in time with the CREATOR and in that conversation, I came to understand deliverance vs. escape. I realized the power and responsibility to set myself free did not belong to any other human being. I was and had always been equipped for freedom! Faith was and is my security harness. JEHOVAH was holding the rope, the strength of the rope and the cushion of the mat below me.

Year ten, courage stood with Faith in declaration that I had finally had enough of misery and rebelling. So, on June 19, 2012 I stood in front of the Judge with my clear request for a divorce. I will never forget the Judge looking over the top of his glasses at me.

As if I was his daughter, he said, "Mrs. Thomas, ten years and all you want is the house and agreed upon child support?" Then asked, "Is there anything else you want to tell me Mrs. Thomas". I looked him directly in his eyes and said, "No Sir, I just want to be done".

With the granting of my divorce I was determined to take back my life and give my daughter the best example of true love for one's self and courage that I could. To void the guardianship authorities and reclaim authority over myself, I had to do what most of us never want to do. Look at the woman in the mirror and determine what vices held me.

I had to come to terms with my faults, lack of account-ability, and my part in holding those vices in place. That alone can be enough to deter someone from real deliverance. That is when your Ear to hear; your inner spirit that guards your seed of Faith takes center stage. Looking at your own ugly: A word said or not said, or an action done or not done can curdle your vision of your character like spoiled milk.

True deliverance is going after the root and requires accepting divine intervention. It is accepting that intervention in whatever form The Creator sends it. My intervention did not come overnight. It came in stages that tested me to the very core of my beliefs and tolerances.

Through the aggravation, broken heartedness, ignorance, selfishness, insecurities, betrayals, confusion, beguiling, and lies of each phase, I learned what I was willing to accept from others and myself. I learned gratitude for what I had made it through. I gained clarity of what image I wanted to project to my daughter and the world.

Through my eye of experiences I wanted to show what healthy Faith, self-love, courage, and well-adjusted loving relationships can look like. I just wanted what everyone else in the world wants. Happiness! Though it looks different to everyone.

Like most, I thought happiness was something you had to go out and find. Strictly in my opinion, that is the biggest misconception of all time. This is what I learned in my phases of chaos. To achieve happiness, you only need to be lined up, ready and willing to receive it.

You are saying to yourself right now, "Yeah right!" "Lady you're full of it!"

So, let me tell you how I prayed for it and almost missed out. On being in line to receive my second chance at true love and being that example of a healthy life that I spoke about a few lines ago. Once I finally accepted me for me and accepted responsibility for me in and out of my mess. I had a different conversation with my CREATOR, in which, I must summarize and tone down the wording just a smidgen because I had a bit of a tantrum.

With kicking and stomping of my feet, I said to GOD, "I'm tired of this". "I don't want to become a bitter old woman and alone". "I'm tired of insecure men that don't respect my worth". GOD, in true ultimate parent form, curved my attitude with this simple question. "What do you want?"

Being that I was out of time but in time, like I told you about earlier. I know I had heard what I heard. So, I stopped pouting and said,

"I want a man that loves You". "I want him to love and care for my daughter as though she were his own". "I want him to love me for me". "Loves my strength, works with me and respects my worth". "And race is like a bag of Skittles, just taste the rainbow". So, he does not have to be black, and height doesn't matter either". "I need for he and I to be able to grow and build together. "I want that perfect husband for me and father for my daughter". "I want to be ready for him and for him to be ready for me". "And please make it feel completely different than what I've ever felt". "So, that I know it's right".

Then I heard, "Be ready!"

After that, I constantly prayed, "Lord, let me be ready". "Don't let me miss him and don't let him miss me".

If I recall correctly, it had to be about two years after that before my Boaz showed up in my path. I had stopped saying, "Let me be ready" and was just praying, "Don't let him miss me and don't let me miss him".

I had become ready because I was actively addressing my own issues. I allowed GOD to put me on the anvil even though I knew it would hurt. When the time came to meet my Boaz in person I tried to renege. I had gotten comfortable with knowing the blessing was coming. But forgot, I still had to walk to it to receive it.

The day of our first date I was getting off work at 8 P.M. but at about 6 P.M., I started feeling sick to my stomach. My close female co-workers knew I had a date and whom it was with. So, when they spotted me moping about they simultaneously turned into the "you are going on this date" cheer squad. Even with their support, I wanted to back out.

But right before I was about to clock out my co-worker, Ms. K, said something to me that shook my spirit. She came to the counter where I was, looked me in my eyes and said, "Get Out of Your Box, before you miss your blessing!" I knew at that moment scared or not I was going because if this was him, I was not going to let fear cause me to miss him.

In May of 2015, my Boaz and I became a couple. In October of 2018 we became one as Husband and Wife. I can honestly say that I know love can hurt. But I now know how good love can feel.

Six months or so before my love proposed to me, my

daughter started calling him Daddy. Then the day he proposed, we were on vacation in St. Louis attending my family reunion. We visited the St. Louis Arch. At the top, directly in the middle of the Arch he proposed to me in front of my Mom, his Mom, my Dad, and my Daughter. Unfortunately, his Boys were not able to attend the trip.

When we came back down to the lobby area there were twelve Orthodox Jewish priests standing around the lobby. What made it even more serial is that they were standing in a large circle with the head priest standing in the middle like they were waiting for us. My Boaz's Mother spoke to a young priest that appeared to be their guide.

She explained to him that my love had just proposed and of course I accepted. She then asked if the head priest would say a blessing over us. Without hesitation the head priest said yes and motioned for us to come forward. Before the excitement of being engaged had even settled in ELOHIM blessed our union.

You will bask in Freedom. Once you realize that no matter what your current issues or circumstances may look like right now, or how they may have looked in the past, you are good ground. You dictate your worth and how your worth is defined.

Understand deliverance versus escape. The power and responsibility to set yourself free does not belong to any other human being. You are and have always been equipped for freedom! Work with the CREATOR to pull your mess out by the root so you can heal. And finally, never let fear be bigger than your Faith in GOD. Your Second Chance at happiness is right in front of you. Line Up and Be Ready!

YOUR TAKE AWAYS FROM THIS CHAPTER

4

DOUBLE FOR YOUR TROUBLE

Torri Eugene

"…The Lord gave me what I had, and the Lord has taken it away. Praise the name of the Lord!"

-Job 1:21 NLT

This story begins on October 10, 2006. That's the day I found out I was pregnant. I just remember thinking "Oh my God, how am I going to tell Spankz?" You see, Spankz was my uncle's childhood friend who I had been sleeping with on the low, off and on for the last six months. He had made it very clear that I wasn't supposed to let anyone in on our secret.

I would later come to find out that the main reason for that was because he had a whole squad of sideline lovers and apparently, we all hung out with each other. However, I soon realized that he was the least of my troubles.

I was living with my Uncle Rich at the time and he only had one rule, DON'T GET KNOCKED UP!!! I kept this secret the best I could because I had to find a way to break the news without getting thrown out. Plus, I knew I had to tell Spankz first so that he could brace himself for the aftermath from his best friend. This plan would soon explode in my face.

It was on a Thursday and I was about to hit the three months pregnant mark. I was lying around the house watching TV with my uncle and some of his friends when all of a sudden I felt my entire insides getting ready to erupt from my body. I ran faster than I had ever done in my life.

"Man, Kat what's wrong with you?" my uncle said looking at me as if he somehow knew I was pregnant and was just waiting for me to be honest with him. At first, I tried to act like I couldn't hear him, but the tactic only made him get upset with me faster.

"Yo Kat, I know you hear me. What the f@#@ is wrong with you?" I had decided that I could no longer lie to the man who had loved me like his very own daughter. I looked him in the face and replied, "I'm pregnant."

I immediately tried to clean up the mess I just made by uttering these words, "I know who the father is. I'm just trying to figure out how I'm gonna tell him. I…"

"Girl you better be playing with me", his face looked as if he had seen a ghost. I could clearly see that he was completely disappointed in me. However, this roller coaster ride hadn't even left the docks yet.

"Man, Rich she probably don't even know the dudes name for real. I told you she is out here just giving it to all who will take it." This was coming from my uncles' little brother, who, to this day, I really don't deal with. I have forgiven him, but I have no need to communicate with him.

"I do too know his name," I fired back at him, "only hoe you know is that chick you dating." I was infuriated by this point in the conversation because for the last 45 minutes I have been called a hoe, slut, and tramp by my uncles and his friends all because I wouldn't tell them who the father was.

"Wait a minute. Did you just say that we know this baby's father?" My uncle looked like I just slapped him into a whole new trance with that statement. "Yes, you do!" I snapped back not realizing that it was my uncle who said that to me.

"It's Spankz baby!" Oh no, my heart pounding in my throat because I wasn't supposed to tell anybody what we were doing and now, not only did my uncle know, but now two of his messy friends do too.

Remember, I wanted to be the first to tell Spankz about me being pregnant, but I hadn't seen him since I found out. I began to try and think about how I could fix this, but my plans got tossed away by the stupidest thing I had ever heard in my life.

"You don't plan on keeping that baby, right?" My uncle had said this as if I had no kind of choice in the matter. My mind cleared up so fast. How do you ask someone a question like that?

"Of course! Why wouldn't I keep my baby?" I asked.

"Because the daddy ain't gonna help you. Kat, you know how that nigga move around. You really think that he gonna be a father to some seed you carrying? You trippin'" stated my uncle.

"So, you telling me that because the father is no good, I should kill my baby? Man, that's not gonna happen. This baby is a gift from God," I proclaimed.

"So is God gonna give you a place to stay because I told you I didn't care what you did as long as you didn't get pregnant."

At this point in the conversation, I was tired, and I looked at my uncle and I told him, "Look a lot of people _____, but not everybody gets pregnant. If God chose me to have this baby, there's a reason."

I packed up my bags and I left. I had nowhere to go but I knew I couldn't stay there. The streets of New York City became the new home for my unborn child and me. I stayed with friends, when I could. I ended up in a homeless shelter that was for young adults on the streets called Covenant House. My best friend, Aaron would check up on me making sure I was eating but the city life was no place for me.

When my mom got wind of what was going on, she got me a ticket to Atlanta, GA. I had my daughter on May 1, 2007. I named her Arianna Neveah Strickland. She reminded me of Duckie from the movie, The Land Before Time, so that became her nickname. I thought that I had it made, but little did I know that the roller coaster was just preparing to leave the platform now.

You see? At the time my mother was married to a man we will call Mister. Mister wanted children and my mom had her tubes tied when she had my youngest sibling. However,

Mister was determined to have kids so he would sneak and have sex with me and told me if I ever told my mother what was going on, he would put me and my child on the streets. Well, he wasn't bluffing.

In the beginning of all this, I thought it was cool. I'm not proud of this, but at that time in my life I was still mad at my mom for "abandoning me" and I felt like this was my way of getting her back. Thank God for repairing my relationship with her. She is now my closest friend.

Nevertheless, back then I wanted her to hurt the way I felt she hurt me. After a while, I realized that the only person that was getting hurt was me. I eventually got tired of the mess going on with Mister, so I decided I needed to go, rather than allow him to put me out. So, I jumped houses with my daughter staying with so-called friends.

Around the time Duckie was 6 weeks old I had met this guy and we dated off and on, so when he heard what was going on with us he convinced his mom to allow Duckie to come stay with her so that she wouldn't have to be on the streets with me. I didn't mind this because I knew she would never agree to allowing me to reside with her again; however, she loved my child like her own. Duckie was about 10 months old.

So, Duckie goes with his mom and I lost my mind. Hunni, I was young and dumb, period point blank. I was in the club every weekend. Hanging out at all hours of the night. Sleeping in abandoned houses, parking lots, etc. I was smoking weed and drinking like I didn't have a care in the world. In my mind, his momma had my number and she would call me if she needed me.

I missed Duckie's first birthday party because I was so hung over from partying that I overslept. Man, I was a wreck but as we know all good things must come to an end. The roller coaster was about to drop.

While I was doing all that partying, I lost my phone so I had persuaded this guy to drive me to my ex's mother's house so I could see my baby. I pulled up to the house to find a 'for rent' sign on the yard. I immediately started panicking, "Where is my baby?" I asked my ex the moment I heard his voice on the phone.

"With my mother, Torri. Why are you tripping? When you needed her help, she helped you with no questions asked and now you acting like she is the bad guy." I knew in my heart that he was right. For two weeks, I tried to reach out to her, but she had changed her number.

I remember having a conversation with my mom, "What you need to do is put out an amber alert," exclaimed my mom, who never liked his mom.

"I can't do that because she was the only one willing to help me in my time of need. She could go to jail and I'm not doing that." To this day I wonder if that was a smart move, because this is where the roller coaster took its plunge.

Three days after talking with my mom, I was able to get in touch with my ex's mom through a mutual friend from her church. Our friend informed me that she had to move due to an issue with the landlord and that she had moved to

Griffin, GA. She said that she tried to call me when I missed Duckie's first birthday but couldn't reach me.

Her health was getting worse and she needed me to pick her up because she couldn't do it anymore. We made the arrangement for me to pick her that Sunday at church. Hell broke loose on Friday.

"May I talk to Torri Strickland?" would be the question that would haunt me for the next three months to come. They came from a social worker for CPS in Spalding County. They were calling me to inform me that Duckie had been placed into their care because his mother had fainted in the supermarket and they couldn't release my baby to anybody who wasn't blood related to her.

This roller coaster had not only dropped but it was hitting the corners rough.

I had failed a drug test; I didn't know that the weed I was smoking was laced with cocaine. I felt betrayed by those who I thought I could trust. To this day I haven't smoked weed since then.

Within the next six (6) months, I was told how irresponsible I was for leaving my child with someone who I knew was ill; however, I had no idea she was sick. No one did. That opened the door for all kinds of attacks on my character. The day I remember crystal clear is December 23, 2008. The day they terminated my rights.

I often joke that I know exactly how King David felt when he realized that there was nothing he could do to save the first child that Bathsheba gave birth to. I had just gotten off the witness stand and had been roasted about how in the 20 months my daughter had been alive that I only actually been a "mother" to her for nine months.

I felt like I was beaten, and I could barely stand up. I just remember running to the bathroom and crying and yelling at God. "Why won't you help me? How can you love me and let me go through all this pain? Will it ever end? You're always taking people from me? I hate you!"

I ended up losing my daughter to the system and I became upset with the world. I blamed everybody for my losing her. I blamed my mom for marrying Mister. I blamed my ex and his mother for moving with my baby and not telling me. I blamed my friends for not telling me that they laced their weed with cocaine. I blamed everyone but me.

I became a bitter woman, but God never left my side. I point that out because we seem to think that just because we are upset with God that He will leave us. That couldn't be the furthest thing from the truth.

Even in my anger God still showed Himself to be on my side. Duckie had been placed in foster care and my biggest fear was that she would forget me. Well I decided that I couldn't let that happen. Her foster mom, at the time, had sent us a picture of her so that I could know that she was ok. She really wasn't supposed to, and to this day I'm convinced that God did that for me.

On the Christmas of 2009, I used 411 to look up the lady's phone number and I called her. When she answered the phone I said, "Look I understand if you say no, but I really miss my daughter and I just wanted to know if I could talk to her." She sighed and then replied, "Being that it is Christmas, I'll allow it, but please make it quick."

I was afraid that Arianna had forgotten who I was and I was so afraid to talk to her. When she came to the phone and heard my voice, I lost that fear. "Mommy!!" she was so excited to hear my voice. I still remember what she got that year: it was a dollhouse, my size Barbie and some clothes. That was the perfect gift that year.

Arianna was moved from that home due to that incident. The lady was hurt but assured me that she would do it again. That event also was the beginning of my healing process. I realized that I had to accept the role I played in this series of events.

Early 2010, I ordered the manuscript of my case. Man, that was the hardest pill I ever had to swallow. In it were the notes from the therapist I had to see in the beginning of the case. I remember when I talked to her, I tried to give her all the perfect answers, but clearly, she saw right through all my lies.

It was after I read that manuscript that I was able to accept my role in all events that took place and I got angry with me. I had decided that I was never going to be a mother again and that I had no one to blame but myself.

That was what I thought, because I am human, so I think like a human. Thank God he doesn't think like me. The bible says that we may think we have a plan, but God is truly the one in control.

During the fall of 2010, I started going to Gordon College, now known as Gordon State College, to get my associates in Social Work. I lived on campus because it was in Griffin and I didn't have a car to commute. However, on certain weekends I would come stay with my family in Atlanta. I had to take out a loan to stay on campus and was paying it off by doing work-study.

By the end of the semester I still owed the school some money so I decided that I would go spend some time in New York City. By this time my uncle and I had reconciled our relationship, and I got a job there to help pay off the debt.

Double Down

On May 1, 2012, as I celebrated Duckie's 5th birthday on my uncles couch, I found out I was pregnant. The child's father stated he wanted to be apart of the baby's life, so I moved back to Atlanta.

At the time, I kept hearing this small still voice say "double for your trouble" but I didn't pay it any attention. I got into a huge blow out with the baby's dad the day before I was to have my first sonogram so I asked my sister if she would go with me. She agreed and we went.

Now from the moment I found out I was pregnant, I felt I was going to have a boy; mostly because I never got sick like I was with Duckie. I kept hearing "double for your trouble" the entire time.

I remember sitting in the waiting room with my sister and saying, "Wouldn't it be funny if I were having twins?" She looked at me and was like, "Not at all." We go back to the room and while doing the measurements the nurse announced I was having twins.

"Is it funny now?" my sister asked. Honestly, I didn't find the humor in that at all. I did, however, feel a sense of peace about it.

I shared this story because you may not have lost a child, but you have probably lost a loved one, a job, a spouse, the list can go on and on. The first thing you may have done was questioning God on why He let it happen to you, but you know what I have come to find out? Losing Arianna was the best thing that ever happened to me. Now let me clear up what that means.

If I would've never lost my daughter, I probably would have been buried six feet underground right now, in jail somewhere, or even strung out on drugs. God used my daughter to get my attention because I was out of control.

I would be lying if I said I don't wish I would've gotten myself together before I lost her, but I know that one day I will be able to share my story with her. What I do know came from this loss is that I have been able to become the God fearing, God loving woman I am today because of it. I thank God that He loved me enough to change me and not leave me the same.

"All things work together for the good of those who love Him and are called according to His purpose", this scripture, Romans 8:28, is what this story is an example of in this chapter of my life.

I pray that you read this and realize two things. One: Come what may, God is always there for you; you just have to call out to Him. Two: Know that if God takes something from you, it's because He has something better in store for you.

Be blessed and may the love of God keep you safe.

YOUR TAKE AWAYS FROM THIS CHAPTER

73

5

UNRAVELING TREASURES

Monica Washington

(Written from my teenage voice)

"Well, well, well. Smelling yourself, are you?"

"No" I replied, walking off as Marcus rudely shoved me into the center of the basketball court.

"Hey, look you guys. Ugly Miss Duck thinks she's all of that with her ashy self". "Yeah so do your mama with her everybody channel self" (key code for slut).

Here I am, Keisha. Fourteen (14) with my lil sis Cayden and her silly friend Star and two of the ugliest, funkiest, rudest boys I've ever met! About to literally go toe to toe with Markus cause he just won't shut up. Somehow Kenny Ray convinced me to stop, and made Marcus apologize. From that day forward, we were the High Five.

Always together doing any and everything. Skipping school, drinking, sneaking into the kiddy clubs and yes, having sex! Markus and I were just that close. Here I am acting like I'm grown with no care in the world, living free. Skipping school by day and sneaking with Markus at night. Till he grew tired of me and decided to sleep with everyone and I mean "errbody".

Little did I know one everyone in the same circle of girls would be carrying Markus's child. Wow here I am 14 and pregnant. All alone. How do I tell mama? How do I tell her that Markus says it's not his?

Any who, I have to and I did.

My mama was one of those "I'd rather you do it at home than in the street" type of gals. Everything but sex. You can smoke, drink, play dominoes, and even have a group of friends over. Yeah our house was the teenagers' playground. But sex was NOT a go.

Heart beating fast. Hands sweating. Throat super tight. "Mama I'm pregnant. Markus says it's not his!" The look in my mother's eyes was unusual. She was very happy and showed it. She told all her friends and everyone who would listen. She even bought me some fat girl clothes, aka maternity, and I was happy and not alone.

I was ready to be a mother to my baby. Four months in and I'm eating good. I'm touching my clothes and spreading and glowing. Then it happened.

My stomach was hurting and I began to feel dizzy. Throw up went through the deep cracks of the couch and floor. They called the ambulance and all I remember was flashing lights and sirens, and my dad saying it's okay.

Hitting every speed bump there was in little old Waco we were finally here at the hospital. Still in pain in this cold room with about five (5) doctors, they rushed me to another bed.

I could hear the doctors asking each other questions. As they undress me from head to toe, they put me in the weirdest gown I had ever seen. "Really, what are you doing down there?"

Snot and tears everywhere, one doctor shaving my harriet while two others are holding my hands and legs. Another one is roughly pushing my gut, feeling for a heartbeat that once was that was no more. Yes sadness arose. Hurt and a different level of pain.

I lost my baby. They called it stillborn. The longest three (3) days of my life it seemed. I called him Andre as the nurse asked what I would like to name him and handed him to me. I held him for a while. I dressed him. I combed his hair. He was so cold and precious. He looked asleep and amazingly peaceful.

Wow, there went me being a mother or so I thought. Job 3:16 says "or why was I not as a hidden stillborn child, as infants who never see the light (ESV)." I still can't make meaning of that scripture but my Lord knows I went to a dark place.

Keisha was not that same little teen that felt free. I actually felt lost and abandoned and you guessed it, lonely, to the point where I was using drugs, sleeping with married men and not leaning in the direction of the light of Jesus Christ, as referred to in John 8:12.

So one could say wild and out of control. A busybody. And they would be telling the truth. I hid my pain and hid it well! I was the type of gal who did drugs and kept myself up. I also sold drugs and made a killing!

I had all types of clientele from black to white, old, young, middle class and poor. I had people like mailmen and Soldiers. It was a whole new level for me.

I remember getting so high I was outside in broad daylight, naked, at one of my main licks house enjoying the air, and clearing my mind at the same time. "Hmmm" I thought as I went back in the house. I took a warm shower to come down. It was the grace of God no one saw me in my naked state.

I mean I did have a reputation to keep even in the street. My name was well known but in a good way. I was Keisha aka Keish and everyone wanted a piece of my pie. But I was very selective in whom I gave it to. I had four mains (johns) that took good care of me. Then I had Soldiers that use to pay just to look at me in lingerie because I was too young to touch.

I was paid well from both husbands and wives. One creep paid me just to take a shower with his wife who couldn't keep her hands off my body. I went over there twice but then it got uncomfortable.

They were arguing over who would have fun with me first. Secret between you and me…it wasn't fun at all. It was just something to do for more cash! Besides I got some of my product for free.

They had so many drugs I was dropping off quarter pounds aka cuties every 2 to 3 hours or half cookies. He was ok with giving it to me because he enjoyed what I was giving him in return.

This was the life one would kill for in the streets and I was living it! Still under my mother's roof, I had to be wise enough not to show her the real, especially Coltan. Coltan was 22 years older than me and had a swagger most men would die for. I mean he had cars, money, charm, fresh white teeth and words that would talk you straight out of your panties.

He wanted me and as sure as pancakes are fluffy, I wanted him but was scared to allow him to see me look his way. Nice piece of chocolate he was but mama said what looks sweet was not always good. Unlike other teens, I made up my mind not to listen to no one at that time. And I went for it.

"Hello, I would like a snow cone please."

"Anything else?"

"No thank you. Oh my god I'm so sorry" as Coltan and I rubbed against each other.

"No problem. What's your name?"

"Keisha."

As his eyes grew huge, he was looking back and forward making sure the coast was clear.

"I'm Coltan, next time be careful. You don't want that soft body of yours getting hurt."

"Hurt? Please I might want to get hurt, besides I like pain!"

"Do you." he said with a silky smile.

"Here. Take my number, give me a call tomorrow."

"What time?"

"Let's say about 5:30."

"Ok."

"For real I would like to get to know you better if that's ok."

"Mmmmm ok!"

I couldn't wait to see Coltan. He was the only thing on my mind. I already had in mind what I was going to wear, my red sexy spaghetti shirt and daisy dukes. Yeah, that's right, something that says hello! Finally morning, wiping the sleep from my eyes, all I can think about was Mr. chocolate Coltan.

Let me get up wash my face and brush these teeth of mines, lord knows I'm ready to start my day. Dang no cereal, oatmeal it is. After watching Ricky Lake and Montel Jordan, it was still only 1:00pm. "Man, where is 5:00 at? (ring, ring) "Hello?"

"Hey, who is this?"

"It's Markus."

"What the heck you want?"

"I want to hangout."

"Hangout?"

Now you guys remember Markus. Yes the low life that said that Andre was not his and left me all alone for 14 hours giving birth to my stillborn child and remind you the one shop cat that everybody knew.

"Boy I don't want to hangout with you. Are you out of your meds? Like seriously, why would you think such a thing? Are you stupid? And how did you get my number?"

"Keisha come on. I'm trying to make it better and why do it matter how I got your number?"

"You shole right Markus, it don't." (click)

As I hung up the phone and immediately blocked his number, I thought he got balls bigger than grapefruit thinking he can make anything better. But Coltan can.

Hey my movie *They Would Not Tell* is on! I must've been really tired, dozing back off just to wake up at 5:15. I rushed to get dressed, brushing my teeth and washing my face again. It was 5:45.

"Oh my God" as I freshen up, I was mad at myself for sleeping so long. But it should still be cool, at least it's not six o clock yet. (Ring, ring, ring)

"Hello, hey I thought you wasn't going to call."

"I told you I would. I was just had something to do."

"Oh ok. So can you get out?"

"Yes I can get out."

"Cool! How about you meet me at the store down the street. But it's going to take me about 15 minutes".

"Ok I'll be in my black caddy, just get in when you make it".

"Ok see you soon".

"Ok."

Wow I'm about to hook up with Coltan. I twisted down the hot street ducking any and everybody praying no one saw me. Yes I'm here thirsty, hot and sweaty but here, as I approach the caddy, butterflies arise. I'm very nervous but somehow I manage to open the door.

"Hey you! How are you?" Coltan asked.

"I'm ok and hot."

"Yes its like 80 degrees. Would you like a drink?"

"Yes, but not from here. Too many people in there I know."

"Oh ok I'll stop at the other store by where we're going."

"Where are we going anyways?"

"Well it's this house I'm working on and its private. I thought it would be a nice quiet place to get to know you."

"Dang I forgot my pill" I thought as I watched his lips move up and down. They looked so delicious. I mean

I could kiss him right now.

"What would you like to drink?"

"Dry wine."

"Really? That's interesting."

"What do you like to do Mr. Coltan besides picking up young girls."

"Wow straight to the point. I like that. But for your information I don't like picking up young girls."

"So why did you pick me up?"

"Cause you're different. You are quiet and always by yourself. And very attractive. So I decided to try my luck."

"Mmhmm. Dang this house is huge. Who house is this?"

"Just one of my contractors."

"Wow that's cool. I thought you were a drug dealer."

"What me? Oh no baby I work."

"So do they."

"Yeah you could say that but I do legal work. And just cause you see me over that way don't mean I sell drugs."

"Yeah I guess" as he removed a small clear bag full of white stuff with a straw in it and began to sniff it.

"What in the world are you doing?" I asked.

"Nothing. Come on, let's get out."

Wow it's beautiful inside as Coltan began to hug me from the back. And I could feel you know what begin to rise. He slowly kissed my neck and whispered in my ear.

"Are you ok?"

A yes rolled off my lips. As his finger traced my lip lines I moved forward and asked him for something to drink.

"Of course. What would you like? Beer wine or a shot of yak?"

"I'll take a cup of wine with ice please" as Coltan sniffed some more of the white stuff.

"What is that?" I asked and he poured some on my breast and gently kissed it. And put some in my nose. And I liked it. I liked how it made me feel. I stopped him, "Wait we don't have a condom and I'm not trying to have kids."

"We good" he whispered, "I can't have no more kids."

So we carried on with sex and drugs. I had everything I needed so I decided to just chill, do me, and get high and fly.

One hot day I just did not feel right and the dope just was not as good as it used to be. I felt very weak and tired and there I went throwing up again and again and again! I'm a person who absolutely hates throwing up. It scares me and I get claustrophobic seriously.

As the room began to spin I remember praying, "God, please, please" and the room slowly slowed down and I was able to get to the hospital. After what seemed hours of waiting and me peeing in a tiny cup the doctor had a diagnosis. I was 8 weeks pregnant! Yes again, but this time I was not happy at all.

I did not want a child. Besides I was trying to survive myself. And Coltan lied to the point I lost respect for him. I also stopped meeting up with him. I was disgusted that I was carrying another child especially his. He said he couldn't have kids and he was married.

I tried different things to lose this unraveling treasure. I punched myself several times and once I even stuck a hanger you know where and nothing worked. "Have mercy Jesus" is what I thought and that's actually what He did.

He had mercy on me and allowed me to love again. Hope and dream again. God blessed me with another son; Keyon, to be exact and I tell you as the nurse brought him to me wrapped nicely in his blanket I began unraveling one of my many treasures.

God knows his own and I'm very grateful for my stinky man. Blessed to have a faithful, loving and just God who always had me even when I didn't have myself.

My heavenly Father has such a way of working. After losing Andre I lost myself and God rescued me just like the sheep that was lost in Luke 15: 3 and showed me a better way, His way of living, loving and helping others. God gave me a second chance and I took it.

God delivered me from drugs and sleeping around and made me one of the best mothers you will ever meet. I am now married to a loving, caring man as well.

To all you young girls who think you're all alone and unworthy: I'm here to tell you, you're not alone! The Lord says in Deuteronomy 31:6 God never leaves you nor forsakes you. Just like God has been with me, so He is with you.

Mothers believe me: I know how easy it is to get caught up in the cares of the world, not knowing what step to take next. I'm here to tell you it's okay to let go and let God. Trust him and He will direct your path and provide. He'll also allow you to be a wonderful mother and the woman you need to be for your children.

If you don't take anything else from me or my story please take God, and allow Him to be your redeemer. He can save you from yourself and bring you to the marvelous Light 1 Peter 2:9b. He is a good Father and A God of second chance!

Stay encouraged, be strong and remember God is in control! God saw fit to give me a second chance so remember everyone wants to go first. It's ok to enjoy second, especially if it's a second chance.

YOUR TAKE AWAYS FROM THIS CHAPTER

6

I'M NO LONGER THAT WOMAN

Sistah Soldier

*Y*ou know the woman who used to claim victim from the inside out. The woman who allowed the opinions of others to guide her life as though they were a part of her future. The woman who didn't know how to Love herself first so she could Love others, and to her own self be true. You see? It took me awhile to gather who I am. Perhaps, even 10, 12, or maybe 20 years to discover the gift of the experiences of my Soul Curriculum™, which brought me to this moment.

Lost Identity

I remembered the days of feeling as if I had to have him by my side (him, being my ex-husband, and any other man I

91

drafted as my Mr. Forever). I was promiscuous, damaged, and wanted to be loved. I wanted to be appreciated, and felt the love of a man would be the coal needed to burn my fire. I didn't know how to love myself, honor myself, or be faithful to me. My life was stuck.

Yes, I had a close relationship with God. Always praying and seeking His face, but somehow it seemed as if I was only moving in a circle while my dreams became a hit or miss. I couldn't understand how God was moving in my life.

When I thought He wasn't concerned or didn't hear me, He was there all the time in a still quiet voice. There were whispers like "I got you. Greater is He that is within you than he that is within this world (1 John 4:4 KJV), trust in the Lord with all thine heart and lean not to thine own understanding (Proverbs 3:4 KJV), and I've never seen the righteous forsaken, nor his seed begging bread (Psalms 37:25 KJV)" ringing in my ears all the time.

These were crucial verses I've learned to quote throughout my life. I never imagined they would become a raft and save me from the sea of worldly living and forgetting I have a divine connection with God.

I was allowing the experience of being abused to become the leader in the community of my life and was ashamed to look up and face the truth of who I'd become. In my culture, women deny abuse because we'd appear as weak, and the embarrassment is even worse. Soon, the admission of being abused places us in a needy category and wanting sympathy.

I had no idea I'd taken some of those characteristics until I continued to push toward discovering the real me. It wasn't pretty. One minute, I was a "strong black woman" and the next, I was throwing myself a pity party and wanted everybody to get in the boat with me and take a cruise.

I didn't know how to create a momentum of continuous actions that lead to one success after another, because during intermission of achievements I'd go back to the old habits of feeling unwanted, scared, and ashamed. My confidence turned on and off like a light switch in a room with multiple occupants.

Living a rollercoaster life, I became internally complacent. How could I be so successful, and yet behind closed doors, I felt so alone, broken, depressed, and unworthy? Why would people choose me to work on projects or something significant? I wasn't worthy. So, I thought.

I wouldn't allow my brokenness to become healed. I didn't know how to. There were no real examples before me. Most women I knew just stayed in the situations they were experiencing because it was their lifeline. They had nowhere to go and no one to assist them with creating a new life.

I began reading a lot of self-help magazines and books that would help me to recreate my life. I'd have my own private "Girlie Days" pampering myself to building my self-esteem. I had none. I was starting from ground zero with everything: internally and externally. So, I worked with what I had in my hands: my bible, Oprah, Essence, Iyanla Vanzant, and God-given skills. That's it!

I looked at myself in the mirror, and all I could see was a young mother who sold out early in life for a make-believe-love. I skillfully wove my life into being a responsible adult at the very young age of eighteen. I leaped into the early motherhood and marriage roles while I was yet discovering myself or affording life to fulfill any of my God-driven dreams or career.

My hallucination was destined to crumble because it wasn't built on a solid foundation. After the walls of deception fell, I had an identity crisis! What was I supposed to do? The fantasy I created was over, and there was no turning back.

Through a dark alley of hurt and pain, I kept searching. I'd lost myself somewhere in the mix and what seemed to be one of my biggest fears became an enormous opportunity for me to reinvent who I had become. If it weren't for my being in the military, I would have been completely bewildered. My position at work demanded my presence and performance daily. I realized its value and how I could use it as a new starting point.

It was all about my relationship. Not with any earthly man, but my relationship with God. Once I understood this, I began to praise God for a second chance of life, motherhood, and career! I had become so many things for so many others but I didn't know who I wanted to be.

If asked, the first thing that would flow out of my mouth were the things I did to make everyone else happy. A Sistah was lost in the mix and couldn't be found.

I thought focusing on what I wanted was a sin and selfish. My mind was being tormented with questions like "how could I only think about what I wanted in life when there were so many others for me to be concerned about (primarily my children and my mother)?

I was the mature one in my family, and everyone looked up to me for answers. It was a lot. Shame masked any emotions I felt and wouldn't allow me to become vulnerable. So, a good portion of my authenticity was held back for the sake of my belief of waiting for the perfect timing. I learned how to create plans to fulfill every one of my dreams in a manner that didn't affect the lifestyle of others and grew closer to God in the process.

("')Ask Him to show you how to decipher through what is not of the truth, and cut anything away from your heart or mind that is not of him, and to help you cultivate those things that lead "to finding your identity, your true self." Luke 9:23 (NIV)

Building from the Ground up

Every step of the way He guided me and I didn't miss a beat. When I felt lonely, I'd study, fast, and pray. I allowed myself to acknowledge my desires for learning new skills. If I thought I wanted to learn Microsoft, I found a class, registered, and then attended. If I felt the need to decorate my home with a new style to represent the awakening me, I did it.

Taking actions that allowed me to express myself helped me to find my voice again. I was teaching myself to go for what "I" liked without judgment. At one point, my apparel was nothing but leopard print. It was as if a tiger within me was waiting to be unleashed, and I was willing to let her be. I gave her the name "Tigress." There was nothing off limits (within reason and if I were financially able of course).

My point: I flowed freely and allowed myself to experience various projects and skills to help me discover what I wanted and whom I wanted to be when I grew up. Through many trials and errors, I learned what I didn't like and that helped me identify what I did like! I expanded myself beyond the box I had created for my life.

God promised me I could do "all things" through Him, and I believed it. I had to know for myself "who" I am. I needed to see the woman in me. I realized I was older and wiser. I was almost thirty years old. Everything was gaining such significance in my life during this period.

The number twenty-nine became one of my favorite numbers and reminded me of the year my life changed. I re-dedicated my life to Christ, and this time, I was all in.

I fell so in Love with His presence; I became celibate. I recognized change was happening within me and on my behalf. It felt surreal. My confidence began to soar.

Lingering Condemnation

However, there was one thing I noticed. Shame was still present. It hung around with intentions of causing disruption. It would allow me to think I was moving forward briskly until it was time for manifestation. I'd work with extreme diligence in producing the visions on the inside of me outwardly but continued feeling as if I didn't deserve it "if" it were to happen.

I would start conversations with influential people that were promising, walk away with high intent to build a relationship, and be too afraid to follow-up fearing I wasn't good enough. So, my response would either be late or not at all. Over and over again, this pattern lived in my DNA.

I didn't have any clue it was ruling my life, because so many other areas were working phenomenally well. However, deep inside, I felt unworthy. Why me? Why would God want to give me riches and glory? I'm nobody. So, I thought!

Shame was a vicious cycle of humiliation that attempted to creep into my life anytime I wasn't consciously aware of who I was becoming, or how I showed up at the moment.

Reinvented for Purpose on Purpose

Since then I've reinvented myself several times. I've implemented new practices in my life to help me be consciously aware of "now" moments. I get to knowingly choose if I'm interested in participating in opportunities, instead of functioning from resistance.

I take time to Love on me through dance, music, photography, and producing meaningful television segments that will inspire the lives of women who are visiting the valley of darkness and disparity needing a raft for life.

You see? I've discovered my self-expression and multiple ways of creating freedom using my voice. I've been there and thank God for a second chance, another opportunity for "living life" with meaningful purpose and intentions! I know my calling in this lifetime, and it's by the grace of God I'm still here to fulfill it.

It's a refining process, and every day gets better and better as I become more and more who He's designed me to be. Life is a revolving door, and I should never settle for where I am now as my forever. I must be ready for what God wants to do in my life at any given moment (using Spiritual wisdom, of course). If I choose not to, I could delay my destiny.

I've learned to own being responsible for my actions, and not blame "others or the devil" for where I am in life. It's a choice. The decisions I make determine the positions I find myself in. Yes, God continues to have Grace and Mercy follow me all the days of my life, but I can't use that as an excuse for not being obedient to His word and fulfilling my purpose.

We each have a purpose and our specific pathway for getting to its fulfillment. No two curriculums are the same.

My Prayer for YOU

My prayer for you is for you to step out of your comfort zone and access life! Grab hold of the truth and begin to live! It's not good enough to "believe" but we must know Love.

Love never blames or judges; therefore, why would we continue to blame ourselves for what happened in our past? It was a learning experience that equipped us with wisdom for the future.

Love is a safe place, and it never stops believing in others. It never accepts failure as defeat. It's not the end of our story. It never gives up, and it refuses to be jealous. Expose the dark areas of your life so you can walk in the light of Love, instead of the residual of confusion, abuse, hurt, and pain.

I know it's easier said than done, but there must be room enough for forgiveness to take place within your heart. Otherwise, there's no room for Love. If we say we Love God, we must trust Him enough to release our truth to Him. He already knows but He wants us to know how much we can trust Him to scale the scars of life and use them for His plans and purposes.

You can't allow yourself to continue being stuck in what was, or what happened, because your "now" awaits you!

It's a second maybe third, or fourth chance.

Take advantage of it. God sent me to tell you He's waiting on you to trust Him with your heart, and His ability to handle your brokenness, unlike anyone else. He keeps His promises and turns the worst experience(s) into the most significant possibilities through LOVE. The greatest commandment of them all is LOVE.

So, Love yourself like never before, and see the world around you light up from the radiance inside of you. It's waiting to be released to change the lives of others who don't understand their experiences until you share yours. That's how it works!

If you're reading this right now, I want to release the favor of God over your life. There is protection over you and your family. Nothing by any means shall harm you, and that as the Love of God overtakes your heart, pain is released and is replaced with joy. You no longer walk with uncertainty, but with boldness and about your Father's business. You're no longer in an identity crisis, but you know who you are and whose you are, and you're willing to go the distance — no more pain. No more discouragement, but peace shall abide with you as you pursue the understanding of your Soul Curriculum™. In Jesus name, amen!

YOUR TAKE AWAYS FROM THIS CHAPTER

7

THE FALL AND RISE

Heidi R. Lopez

Some of us fall… fall flat on our faces. We fall and never have the courage to get back up. Seems as though this life is full of "potholes", would you agree? It's happened to me many times during my life, I'm sure you can relate in some way or another.

Profound Loss

The decade that had one of the deepest effects on me, and made me part of who I am today, was during my twenties. I experienced my first and most impactful loss during that time. I lost a younger sister - Lillian. She was a twin to another sister, and she was only fifteen years old. They were practically my life, as I was the older sister acting on behalf of my mother and father since they worked all the time.

I helped care for them, had them with me anywhere and everywhere I would go. We were very close, we had a very tight bond, and my parents trusted that they were safe and sound when they were with me.

The night that I lost my little sister, we were all out at a family friend's birthday party. The day began very eventfully for my sister, as she was invited to a few other parties that day. It was almost like a treat since she was able to go with friends and didn't have to take me along. By the evening time, she ended up with the whole family at this party.

Everyone was having a good time, talking and dancing amongst one another. We weren't too far from home, so my parents decided that they would go home and leave the twins with me, and I would later drive us home.

I think they did this for a few reasons: one, because they knew the girls would be safe; and two, because I had a new boyfriend. Traditionally, in my family, no daughter dated without a chaperone. I guess they figured the girls would serve as my little chaperones.

Have you ever had to take a sibling out with you on a "date"? As a teenager back then, I didn't appreciate my parents' intentions, but now, I understand that they loved me and were only looking out for me.

My parents drove off, heading home. Yes!!! Freedom!!...

The Unthinkable

It wasn't even five minutes from the time they had left, that all the chaos started. I looked over in the corner of the yard and there was a group of people gathered around someone. I wasn't sure who it was, so I began to scan the yard for the twins but I only spotted one. I ran over with the worst gut feeling I have ever experienced.

Have you ever felt that feeling, your stomach twisting and turning, and full of knots? The feeling of wanting to vomit. Those are just some of the feelings I recall having. Truthfully, the fine details and some of the not so fine details are all a blur to me now. Up to this day, I close my eyes and see only darkness; I cannot see anything from that night or time frame in my life, to be quite honest.

I found my sister down on the ground, having a full-on seizure. What do I do? I tried to roll her over to the side and waited for the seizure to stop. Some friends ran over to her and began to perform CPR once the seizure had stopped. She wasn't breathing and I was terrified. I remember shouting across the yard for someone to call 911.

The ambulance took what seemed to me like forever to arrive. I stayed by her side as everyone in the yard stood still and watched. Everything seemed to move in slow motion. My parents were called immediately and we all rushed to the hospital. I parked my car and ran inside the hospital, looking for my family. The receptionist directed me to an office, where I found my parents, my sister, and a physician.

As I walked in, all I can remember was seeing my mom nodding her head back and forth, saying "no, no", my dad holding my mom, and my sister crying. The physician telling our family how sorry he was for our loss. It all happened so fast.

This was our family's' first immediate loss, and it was all new to us. The thoughts that fill my mind today thinking back are sad ones, and thoughts of how I could never have made it to this point in my life now without God Almighty. My life was forever changed that night, in more ways than you might imagine.

I remember walking into the room where my sisters' lifeless body lay, my mom sitting at her side. What could I tell my grieving mother right now? She sat there in complete silence, staring at my sister.

"She is in a better place now mom" are the only words that came out, but the next few words that she said to me, changed my life forever.

"Shut up, this was all your fault! How could you do this?" was her response to me. Those words, and those words alone, killed my soul that night. "How was I not more careful? How did I let this happen? They trusted me so much with the twins, how could I do this?" That night for me was more than the physical loss of my sister, it was the loss of the mother/daughter relationship I once knew. Life as I knew it was gone, a ghost, nonexistent. My family had fallen apart.

The Love I Searched

A year or so went by after my sister passed away. Time moved on, but the overwhelming guilt remained the same. My mother's words echoed in my head daily. "I did this to my family. How could I destroy my family like this?" I thought.

The other twin was now attending high school, my parents were just existing, and I was working at a bank call center. Things at home were never back to normal; it seemed as though my sister and I only had each other. My mother worked day and night in order to keep busy and my father spent his entire days at my sisters' gravesite.

I felt like the parent because they really weren't there phys-ically or emotionally for us. I was never able to grieve, and I missed being loved. The job at the call center was one of the best paying jobs I had ever gotten so I felt lucky. You see? I worked many fast food jobs and retail stores; in my mind, I had scored and moved up in the working world.

That job led me to a new environment and new people.

This is where I met Mr. Wonderful, or so I thought. This young man was very friendly, quiet at times, very attentive, and a good listener. He was more than willing to help me when I had any questions about the job. He had been working there for about six months more than I had, so he had more experience.

We started as coworkers, and after some time, we began dating. He was interested in taking me new places, buying me things, listening to me, and he made me feel loved. I now know that when you do not make God number one in your life, you'll go out seeking love and acceptance from people and worldly things. The enemy has a way of painting beautiful pictures of darkness and unreal love.

I had the need to feel loved and understood. I was very vulnerable during these years. I searched for love and acceptance in a lot of wrong places. What I saw in front of me at that time was the love I thought I was looking for. All seemed to be going so great in this new relationship. I felt in love. But was love supposed to hurt?

I'm sure some of you may be thinking back on past relationships right now, and how you all had your ups and downs. Every relationship has those, right? I remember one instance where we were headed out on a date, I can't recall where to. He drove and I, of course, was the passenger. He seemed to be a little on edge, but I didn't think it was anything out of the ordinary or anything to worry about.

He asked me a question, and I responded by saying "huh, what did you just say?"

That is all I remember about the conversation. The next thing I know, he was grabbing me by the throat and banging my head against the window. All this continued as he drove around town. At a couple of red lights, he was punching my side and punching my legs. Why does "love" have to hurt? Or does it? That was the first of many beatings I got by that Mr. Wonderful.

The beatings only got worse every time. Red flags you ask? I had no idea about red flags, or signs, or what I should have looked for. I was a young woman, seeking acceptance, seeking unconditional love, all in all, I had no self-love.

In the beginning, he painted my world of beautiful colors and his promises were never-ending. It all sounded like the very things I lacked and was in search of. For the next six months, I endured beatings, verbal abuse, emotional abuse, and even sexual abuse; the list went on and on.

He and I met at one of my very lowest points: I confided in him how much my family and I were dealing with and he used my loneliness and sadness to manipulate me. Looking back, I see that with every detail that I shared with him, he pretended to care and brainwashed me into believing that he was all I had.

He had me believe that I was alone in this world; and, without him, I would never become anything. No one would ever want me. I believed all of it at the time because what I failed to share with you earlier was that fact that he did things to me against my will, and in my mind, I was damaged goods. Not even God could love me now.

"He was right, how could any other man ever want me?" He played with my mind so much so, that after he would beat me, I would end up apologizing to him for causing him to do this to me. Why didn't I just run, you ask? It's not as simple as you think. The guilt, shame, and fear he poured into me made me freeze up every time I wanted to leave.

One day, as we sat in his car parked outside my house, he got upset over something. I knew the drill and I knew what was coming next. I don't know what came over me that time, but after a few punches and slaps on the face from him, I looked at him and punched him back. I feared what would happen next, but I was more scared of ending up dead because of him.

In the moments that I was being beaten, I decided to set myself free. I dug deep and fought back. I wanted to get as far away from him and this miserable life as I could. Shortly after that day, I made my mind up; I was going to the Army.

Finding myself

The road to the military was not an easy one. I had to make a choice of leaving my family behind, but most importantly, leaving my little sister behind and that

caused me great guilt. I was looking forward to finding myself, exploring the world, seeking new adventures. In order to make the decision, I convinced myself that I needed to join the military because I needed some discipline.

I wanted to prove to my family and myself that I could go out into the world alone and make it. I was curious to see what this BIG world was all about. I was a young twenty-three years old by this time and excited about my new journey.

The start of my career was not a peachy walk through the park. It was hard physical work; meeting new people, and being away from my family was extremely difficult. Not trusting anyone was an issue for me, some of the exercises that we did during training involved trusting one another, and so by force, I slowly learned to trust.

I made some good friends, or as we call them, Battle Buddies. I used my family as my motivation to continue and completed Basic Training and Advanced Individual Training as an honor graduate.

Next stop: Schofield Barracks, Hawai'i

How did I get so lucky you ask? I didn't know at the time; I just knew I was in paradise. As a young Soldier at the time, I was looking forward to the same guidance and discipline I had gotten from the more seasoned Soldiers during my initial training. I wanted to become like them someday, hopefully earning rank and moving up the chain of command.

Now I know that this was a young naive mentality because when I arrived at my new "home", everything was different. It was more relaxed than I expected. The senior Soldiers were not as hard on the young Soldiers when they interacted with them, especially if they were good looking.

During my first week there, I was invited by several senior enlisted Soldiers to stop by their barracks room and "hang out". It was very intimidating because I was new, alone, and far from home. Why did I join the military and leave home? I made the choice in part because I was running away from my problems, just to now face new ones.

The pressure was real, and I just wanted to be accepted. The unwanted sexual advances were a part of the deal too. Some preyed on young Soldiers like they were sharks. Should I have accepted and gotten myself into a bad situation, or decline and be on THE list?

Some of these Soldiers were single and some were married but being married did not stop some of them from joining in on the advances. There was a lot of partying and drinking that went on, and if it weren't for battle buddies looking out for one another, I just don't know how some of us would have ended up.

My time in the service was not all bad: I did meet some great friends who have become more like family. I traveled a lot and learned many things, good and bad. When I was 27 years old, I found out that I was expecting. I was still figuring out life at this point and about to become a single mother therefore, I was happy and terrified all at the same time. This would be another life I would have to care for.

What a huge responsibility, but what a tremendous blessing. I must admit that the timing (according to me) was not the best, but God knew what He was doing. That day was the first of many days that I dropped to my knees and cried out to God for his help.

I always knew that God was somewhere out there, but I just didn't feel that he would be with someone like me. Someone who had caused her sister to die, caused a family to fall apart, caused someone to abuse her, and now caused men to prey on her. I didn't even feel worthy of asking God for help, I just didn't deserve it. But by his grace, everything in my life was about to change.

Second Chance

By my twenty-eighth birthday, I was a mother. My time in service had ended and I moved back home with my seven-month-old son. I worried about how I would make it out in the civilian world. Everything seemed so different.

I had a steady income for all those years, and now, how would I make it? God made a way for my son and me. By the time I left my duty station, I was offered a government job and have been there ever since. For many years thereafter, I worked hard to give my son all that he needed and wanted.

I also went through times where money was scarce, where my son was ill and I had no medical insurance, and that scared me. God saw me through it all, yet I never stopped to thank God for what He had provided me with. I never thanked Him for loving me and for all He had blessed me with. All I found myself doing now was complaining and trying to find solutions for myself. I felt like He was punishing me for many bad life choices I had made in the past. God was still not number one in my life.

My Turning Point

When I stop and reflect on my past choices, it scares me to think I once lived without God in my life. I chose to put him last and hoped to make it out in one piece. How could I ever think that way? The enemy has a way of painting a pretty picture, doesn't he? But God has the ultimate power and say over the enemy and over our lives if we surrender to Him. His timing is perfect!

In 2014, I hit another low point in my life; I was battling depression and anxiety. I was tired of fighting an uphill battle with life and decided that I wanted and needed peace for once.

I was fortunate enough to take a trip to the Holy Land that year. It was there, in the holiest of places, that I first felt worthy of God's love. I remember the exact day it happened. I drank living water from the well of Jacob that day and heard the story of the Samaritan woman, and it hit me like a ton of bricks.

God is a merciful God, a loving, and forgiving God. I gave my life to him during that trip. He made me see and feel things that I can hardly describe. God IS real and God loves you and me!! He is always there, waiting for us with His arms opened wide! All we must do is surrender to Him. Even when we do not feel worthy, He is there to love and guide us, just like it says in Psalm 23 (my favorite passage).

I was one of the ninety-nine sheep, scared and lost but He found me. He has blessed me with a wonderful son, a stronger family relationship, a steady job, but most of all, He has blessed me with the unconditional love and for-giveness I searched for. By giving my life to Him, I am learning to love and forgive myself as He has already done. Almighty God has given me a second chance.

YOUR TAKE AWAYS FROM THIS CHAPTER

8

STILL STANDING

Dorlean Washington

Often times when we go through tests, trials, and tribulations many tend to want to give up or even play the blame game. This causes us to lose sight of Jesus and focus on the situation(s) and problem(s) when we should be still and know that He is God (Exodus 14:4). For He is able, He is faithful, and He will fight for us.

I have been given this opportunity to share with you a portion of what the Lord has done in my intricate life's journey. I am eternally grateful that my loving Father has kept me and preserved me. Why, because I desire to be kept by Him. He has uprooted and pulled me out of the clutches of hell and brought me over into the Kingdom of God.

I wasn't raised in Church. My Church was the street of hard knocks. Some of you know what I'm talking about. Somehow I knew to call on God in times of trouble, "God, if you get me out of this I won't do that anymore." Because I am a woman of my word, I didn't do that particular thing again; however, I somehow managed to get into some thing else.

I knew nothing about this man named Jesus and how He died that I may live. I never even heard of His name. My spiritual birth began at the Christian House of Prayer, Copperas Cove, TX where I was graced and blessed to be gifted with Pastors after God's own heart according to Jeremiah 3:15. The late Bishop Nathaniel Holcomb and Pastor Valarie Holcomb will forever be embedded in my heart as my spiritual parents.

Before Christ, I use to pass judgment on Clergy and church folk. Why, because I saw many doing what I was doing in the world; therefore, I had no desire to go to anybody's church. Somewhat like Saul did before God gave him the name Paul. Saul persecuted Christians of the Roman Empire for over two centuries.

The Father knew I needed a clean Pastor who had been tested, tried, proven, lived, and walked the gospel of truth for the glory of God. He had the heart of the Father for saving souls for the Kingdom of Heaven. Bishop Holcomb strived to get people closer to God, not to him. He was a great ensample and example for all people.

When I first came to Texas I was married and worked on the Military installation. The Army was doing cutbacks at this particular time and was offering Soldiers money to get out of the Army. And so, my husband took the money and left me with three children to raise. On top of that I lost the house we were renting.

Even though I had not accepted Jesus as Lord and Savior of my life yet, God provided a ram in the bush. The NCO-IC I worked with was a single woman raising two children. She opened up her home to my children and me. She was an angel in disguise used of God to assist me through my valley experience.

We both ended up working a second job as a bartender some nights, switching off so one of us would be home with the children. Several months had passed, I was divorced and my roommate had purchased another home. It was time for me to stand on my own, but how? I learned all I could by watching her conduct business with the realtor and others associated with purchasing a home.

I used the same realtor my roommate used because she was aware of my situation. This woman told me my credit was too low and I didn't make enough money to purchase the type of home I was looking for. Within the next couple of days, that same realtor reached out to me and said,

"God" put it on her heart to help me to purchase a home. So she started showing me VA repossessed homes.

These homes are placed in the local newspaper and bid on anonymously. You don't know who bids what. Therefore, whoever has the highest bid gets the home. If the home was posted in the newspaper twice and no one bid on it, the third time it is posted the house is placed on a first come first serve basis.

My realtor had her husband spend the night in another city to get my bid in first. During the midst of this transaction, I prayed and called on God to move on my behalf and He answered my prayer. My bid was so low that my mortgage each month would be $350.00, and the favor of God allowed me to win the bid. God gave my children and me a second chance to have a roof over our heads.

I made a promise to God that my children and I would start going to Church on a regular basis. I was so sick and tired of the empty lifestyle I was living. But what do you do when you don't know what to do? You do what you know to do and that is pray! God gave me a second chance at a new life in Him.

Prayers Manifesting

One Wednesday evening I was driving to work to the Disabled American Veterans (DAV), where I was bartending, and a billboard caught my attention "Christian House of Prayer." I slowly proceeded to drive around the filled parking lot. Suddenly I heard a heavenly sound of singing that saturated the atmosphere. As I was drawn in that direction, I had an unction to give a donation to the Church and motioned the parking lot attendant to come take the donation, but he would not.

I felt as though my attire was inappropriate for Church so I did not go inside. As I was leaving the grounds I began to feel a tugging within. Amazingly enough, in that same week, something came over me to the point where I lost the desire and taste for drinking or smoking anymore. Instantly, God took the taste from me without gum or a nicotine patch and I quit both cold turkey.

Sunday came around and I was being torn between going to church and going to work. My spirit man was awakening and my soul was wrestling against it. I decided to dress in modest apparel. Suddenly I heard a soft faint voice saying, "come".

The tugging within grew stronger and stronger. Thoughts of fear and doubt began to enter into the battlefield of my mind. [Should I go to work or should I go to church? If I do not go to work, I will be fired, but I need the money! How would I make ends meet?] Jesus was knocking at the door of my heart.

I chose to go to church as I had promised God. As I entered through the doors into the foyer I was greeted by an older woman who gave me a huge love hug

like she was expecting me. For the first time in my life, I felt genuine love oozing out from a person, with no motive behind it. I had never been embraced with real passion like that in my entire life but God gave me another chance to see that true love does exist.

And so, the usher motioned me to follow him through the double doors into the sanctuary. The Pastor was already in the pulpit preaching. Who is this Jesus the Son of God that the Preacher was talking about? The words he preached pricked my heart and caused me to weep uncontrollably.

Throughout my life there had been a consistent battle of mental and physical abuse, deceit, being lied on and to, talked about, and my character being assassinated. Nevertheless, this trusted voice penetrated the darkness and gave me a light of hope. Then it came, the clarion call for those who were in need of a Savior. My heartbeat became Gods heartbeat and I ran to the altar with hands lifted high, surrendering my life to a true and living God.

In an instant in my spirit, I was born again and felt as though God has granted me a second chance in life. I truly understand the meaning of the scripture when it says, "therefore if anyone is in Christ, he is a new creation. The old things are passed away; behold the new has come into being," 2 Corinthians 5:17 (NAS).

I'm able to see myself and everyone else through His eyes.

Sin had me bound, but the God of a second chance resurrected, redeemed, restored, and revived me through forgiveness and His unfailing love. He lifted the cloud of guilt, shame, and condemnation and gave me a fresh start. He took me to a place where I can be free and do better. This opportunity of newness of life is only found in Him, through which I can live and have life more abundantly.

Does this mean I will sin no more? Of course not because all have sinned and come short of His glory due to the soulish nature. It simply means through Jesus, who bore my sins, took away the sin nature instantly in the spirit, which causes me to be more conscious to sin less. The struggles are still real and there will always be a continuous battle between the spirit and the soul.

I became hungry and thirsty to come to know more about Jesus. I've learned that God has given each of us a definite and distinct purpose to fulfill, designed especially for us as the unique individuals He created us to be. The enemy tried to kill me in my mother's womb, but God said not so. Like Isaiah, the Lord called me before my birth from within the womb (Isaiah 49:1).

My parents may have conceived and given birth to me, but they cannot define me. The only one who can define me is the One who created and designed me.

When people grasp the reality that God calls us before we are born and entered into this world for a specific purpose, it will release the pressure of trying to figure out only what God can work out. God is faithful.

God knows everything about us. He knows our divine assignment before we ever took one breath; He knows everything we have done, the good, the bad, and the ugly; He knows everything we will ever do before we even do it. I was amazed by the truth He revealed to me that was in me. Ask God to show you yourself and the plans He has specifically for you.

God's call is graced based and not work-based. This means I was called before I did anything to deserve it and yet He called me forth anyway. This also means I cannot do anything to disqualify myself from the call, because I did nothing to qualify myself in the first place. That is why He is a God of a second chance and many other chances.

As a single woman I thought I had to be strong in deed. I learned to depend on and ask God for everything in order to obtain His strength so I would not grow weary in well doing. Most of all I desired the Spirit of God to rise up inside me to lead and guide me in spirit and in truth. This required me to die to self on a daily basis, commanding my flesh to come under subjection.

Sin is always waiting at the door and temptation is right around the corner. From the redeemed to the unsaved, no one is exempt from the clutches of evil.

This is why no one should think more highly of themselves or place themselves or anyone else on a pedestal. It is so easy to judge others about the very things we tend to do ourselves.

I recall a time where I was driving my children to school and it was trash day. Someone forgot to take out the trash and for some reason I was very upset about that and began to raise my voice in anger.

Even in the midst of anger, I heard the voice of the Lord say, "I'm getting ready to take some trash out of you." I stopped the car and from the pit of my belly uprooted that spirit of anger and deliverance took place that very moment.

Another time coming from an event, again I was driving and a song came on about being at the cross. It was as if the Holy Spirit took the wheel and the words from that song took me to the place at the cross where I was able to lay all my cares and concerns at the feet of Jesus. Once again the light touched that darkness that had been buried and deliverance took place. I am still standing through the process of healing, deliverance, and growth.

God hates sin and He wants to cleanse us from all unrighteousness. Sometimes it is buried so deep that He has to deliver us a layer at a time. Every day is a new day, a new beginning, and an opportunity for another chance to walk upright in the will of His way. God's love all by itself means we get a second chance and that love extends to all creation.

LET US PRAY

Dear Heavenly Father and Most gracious Lord of Hosts, thank you for giving unto us multiple chances to live this life in You. Though we experience pain, suffering, and the storms of life, You are faithful and just to graciously forgive us, which is only made possible through the powerful blood of Jesus.

We are eternally grateful that we are yet still standing knowing that we still have a purpose in life. Every day we wake up is the gift of another chance. We bless You and praise You, we give You and You alone all the glory and honor. It is in Jesus Omnipotent name we pray. So be it and Amen.

YOUR TAKE AWAYS FROM THIS CHAPTER

129

9

THE PUSH FORWARD:
I AM AN OVERCOMER

Michele Graham, BSN, RN

(Mimi Queen)

*I*t is a great honor for me to be sitting to share my story with all of you! I was born and raised in Africa and my first language is French that I still speak quite fluently. I went to school there in Africa, excelled and joined my country's University at the age of 16. At the age of 23, I started some businesses, traveling all over Europe. After some time I decided to come to America and make America my new home.

In 2000 I emigrated from the Ivory Coast (West Africa) to Dallas, Texas. I left behind my mom, my brothers, sisters and my son. I met some beautiful ladies when I decided to move to Killeen Texas, after I went through a very difficult

131

divorce; but through the divorce, I am able to share my stories to encourage you.

Back Story of arrival in the States

I got married and had two beautiful girls. We were kind of a perfect couple, I thought. There were no fights at least. I put myself in school, learned English first and took some CNA classes.

I worked as a CNA for four years, then went back to school for medication aide. I worked as a med aide for three years and with a couple coworkers we decided to go to school to become Licensed Vocational Nurses (LVNs). I even took the entrance exam. We passed the test but a couple days before LVN school was to start, I decided I was not going to be an LVN. God spoke to me, "It's not your calling". I decided to move forward with my education because of the love and care I have for my patients.

Some of my nurses told me, "We see you as a good nurse. Go for it!" So I signed up and took my prerequisites in Arlington, TX at Terrington College. While doing these classes, a few of my classmates again said we need to go do associates in nursing. God again spoke to me and said don't do it, move forward for bachelors degree in nursing.

I went back and took all the prerequisites needed to apply for the Bachelor of Science in Nursing degree. I first graduated with an Associate Degree in Liberal Arts in 2010. I applied to almost 15 schools, 10 of which gave me an acceptance letter. Some of them were associate degrees and some were bachelor degrees. Again the God of second chances spoke to me and I picked a Christian school, Southwestern Adventist University in Keene, TX, outside of Fort Worth, TX.

My journey wasn't easy because I speak French. I think French, I do everything French and I also have to find somewhere in my mind to translate everything that I'm reading in English to French to understand all my studies: my quizzes, my books and everything. Then I have to re-translate from French to English and write it out. It wasn't easy but God!

While I was there I was blessed to be, not once but several times, on the dean's list! In May 2013 I graduated with my Bachelors of Science in Nursing from Southwestern Adventist University.

I had my first job offer at John Peter Smith Hospital and took that position; that's where I got my basic nursing training. In my young career I was blessed to excel at everything I put my hands to.

After a few months, I had an offer at another hospital, Life Care of Fort Worth. I took that job and was fortunate to work in the Intensive Care Unit (ICU) taking care of critically ill or injured patients there. After a few months in the ICU, I was offered the position of House Supervisor at John Peter Smith hospital.

After working there for some time, I chose to leave John Peter Smith hospital as house supervisor. I wanted to give back to this country in some way for all I'd been able to accomplish here. With that endeavor in mind, I went to work for VA Dallas.

I work for VA Dallas and still serve our large Veteran population up until now. Working for the VA healthcare system is to me, to give back to this country by taking care of those who have defended this country and aided other countries. All my patients are those who served this country.

I praise God because the visionary of this book and some of the co-authors are also Veterans. They put their lives on the line for us to be free so I can say I'm proud when I take care of them as patients and I have them as friends. I am a Charge nurse and have a good team; we work together.

God again spoke to me. He asked me to move forward, even if English is not my first language.

With that unction, I went back to school yet again.

Currently attending Walden University, I am on track for my Masters for Family Nurse Practitioner. I want to say thank you to God because in the midst of everything I went through, I was able to almost complete my Masters for Family Nurse Practitioner.

As I write these words to you I'm on my second rotation with two more to go: Women's Health and Nurse Practitioner Roles. By God's grace, I will be graduating in early 2020 as a Family Nurse Practitioner; and, for me that is a true testimony!

Why all of this matters

A lot of people think because we came from Africa and we came from a French speaking country we cannot push forward.

I was already in my 30s when I came to this country but that didn't stop me. I believe in God who strengthens me and I moved forward.

I guess I need to tell you a little of the background story of my marriage and divorce so you understand.

I got married and had two children. We were together and the way I have been raised is different from what some people do here in America. In Africa, the wife has to work and back up her husband.

By nature I'm a hard worker. Almost my whole nursing career, I always held two jobs. Most of the nurses around me also worked two jobs to help support their families and move forward in their futures. I decided to work those jobs but it took a lot out of me.

I worked night shift then in the daytime I worked in a home health position or part-time at another hospital. About that time I took a traveler nurse position because for me it was bringing more money into the household.

My ex-husband saw it as me not being involved too much in my family's lives. He has a degree; however, out of nowhere he chose to quit his job. According to him, he worked for almost close to 15 to 17 years and he was tired of working so he decided to sit at home.

We had two kids who needed insurance, clothes, food, and a roof over their heads. I stepped in and took the reigns. I was working to make sure everything was okay at home.

It was a big slap in my face. One day I came home from work and he asked me, "How do you see yourself in five years?"

"Pursuing my education."

"How about ten years?"

"Same thing. Pursue my education and also open up businesses because I do not want to die working for somebody else. I have dreams and this country is the country of dreams, American dreams."

That's when he informed me about him filing for divorce. It was a wakeup call.

My family got involved: my brother came all the way from London and another brother came from Africa. My elder sister even came and bowed at his feet, crying on behalf of my family because we don't believe in divorce. To us, it is a shame to be a divorced woman but my ex husband didn't agree with that.

I even reached out to the church, involved the pastors, and reached out to his friends and family. They all tried to talk to him but it was too late.

He said he had a dream and in this dream God told him to divorce me. He said that was his motivation and he didn't want God to punish him. He said he had to obey what God told him in his dream…

Ok, wow. The things we blame on God.

It was heartbreaking.

He made me believe that we would be working things out. While fighting for my marriage, I was trying to make things better. During this time, I went to the doctor and was told I needed to have a major surgery. While at the hospital having this major surgery, my ex-husband didn't even bother to come to the hospital to see me.

His mother brought the girls by. He came only for 15 minutes to tell me that his homeboy was having his 40th year birthday bash in New York and he had to go. I said, "But I had surgery, major surgery and you leave me in a hospital bed going to your homeboy birthday party?"

He said he has to go so I told him to go. After he returned from the birthday party, something happened…

I never went to my ex-husband Facebook page before but the Holy Spirit led me to go there this time. While I was in bed recovering, I was reading and I discovered that it was his ex-girlfriend birthday party that he was attending.

I didn't just assume but heard all the stories about the birthday party happenings. I got up from the bed, went to the office and for the first time in my life I confronted my now ex-husband. He confirmed it was true by saying to me, "Take it the way you want".

Long story short, he was seeing his ex-girlfriend again.

I had moved to sleep in the living room, choosing to stay in the home because of my children.

Soon after this, the divorce was finalized but I didn't even know about it. I never received any letter from the judge. He made me believe that everything was okay but then one day I received a divorce letter.

Because I never went to court, I got charged by default. I lost my house, my children, EVERYTHING. They gave him child support close to $2000 a month.

While I was fighting to put food on the table to make sure that my family would lack nothing, he found time to go to court and tell them I'm a bad mom. But I care about my kids, that's why I was making sure when they travel I bought the tickets, food, anything they needed.

I didn't want them to feel badly around their friends even if their daddy wasn't working for more than two years. I didn't want them to notice anything. I took care of my children and my household.

A couple people told me that if it were them, they would go through depression, and they would make sure to get some psych meds. I never did those things.

I am not on any depression or psych meds (but don't stop taking yours if you are on them. Go see your doctor!)

I find myself deep in my Bible and I find myself deep in worshiping my God. If it weren't for God and the Bible, prayer and meditation, I would not make it.

I share with you guys my nursing journey but I also share my divorce because while I was going through the divorce I was still going to school.

I never experienced depression, anxiety or insomnia. I said the way everything happened in my life, I praise God because He gave me strength every single day. I needed to put food on their table so I was going to school full-time to improve my life but at the same time, work 40 hours a week. While working 40 hours, and school homework, I still find time to praise God. I find time to make A's and B's in my school. It's all about God.

Weeks after I got kicked out from my house, I was on the street. I went to my big sister's house. In the middle of all this, by God's grace, I was able to help my son immigrate to this country, in June 2017. We shared the same bed, my son and I, for almost three months. I told my son to "make mommie proud!"

I told my son that I would love for him to serve this country and he listened! He joined the U.S. Army and is currently stationed oversees. I told him "reach where mommie would never reach." My son has a bachelor's degree in telecommunications from Africa so it had to be transferred here to the states. He is now an Engineer in Telecommunications in the Army and currently getting ready to go to Officer school.

The Way Ahead

After my divorce I relocated to Killeen, TX, a small military town between Fort Worth, Texas and Austin, Texas. Being here has helped me a lot because here I am able to focus on my future. Killeen is not busy, not like in the big city of Dallas.

I was able to sit. I took some time off everything, even time off school for two semesters to find myself. Finding myself, for me, was to go deeper in God with my bible, be more involved in my church, and my prayer life. It also helped me to redirect my life.

It wasn't easy. The bible said I never told you it would be easy but God will never let you down. I experienced that! Every day for me is a testimony.

I never knew how to pay bills during my marriage because where I came from the husband is in charge of all the bills. There are no questions to ask. But being a divorced woman I have now to face reality. I had to make sure my bills were paid. It was a challenge, a new beginning.

On top of everything, I used to be a travel nurse with high pay. I came here and now I'm no longer a travel nurse. I'm now a staff nurse in a smaller hospital, basically a huge pay cut. But I accepted it. I'm not making the money of a travel nurse now but I've been paying my child support of almost $2,000 a month faithfully by God's grace.

I was able to establish myself, get a home and furniture, and get my life rolling in the right direction. God blessed me! He brought someone in my life and he changed my life.

The first thing he did was he asked me to stop working two jobs and he helped me. I call him sent from heaven! He helped me to make sure all my bills were paid. He taught me how to work less and be more efficient. He showed me that there is life after divorce.

I was able to push for my education and reconnect with my girls. My desire is to show them the way, not to confuse them. My desire is to regain custody of my girls.

Advice for women: Do not talk bad about the other parent. Just tell them things did not work out. Explain to them on their level. My girls are now 15 and 12, teenagers so I've been able to share a little bit.

I'm sharing my testimony to all the women who think divorce is the end of everything. No. Divorce is a beginning of what God has in store for you. I see myself as a living testimony of never giving up. Move forward. Push until the last call to meet our Savior.

I strongly encourage all women who read my testimony to know that man is not the end of your life.

God took us from the man's rib to be the partner, the helper. But if the man doesn't want you, it is not the end of your life. Push your sleeves up and wash your hands. Find yourself in the Bible and show to the world that you can do it.

There is so much I could share with you here but it will have to wait until I write again. I will leave you with this:

It hurt but nothing is impossible if you get the best partner and that partner is GOD.

YOUR TAKE AWAYS FROM THIS CHAPTER

10

OVERCOMING BULIMIA

Shanta Green

I guess the question some of you might have is how did bulimia even become a part of my life? Well, as a little girl I was molested by someone close to the family. Too afraid to tell, food became a crutch for me (until) I suppressed the memories. I was so terrified of him.

No one knew what I had been through. Food became a strong part of my life. Food became a coping mechanism for me. I was this chubby little girl with so much hidden pain.

FAST FORWARD

I'm 19 years old in cosmetology school when the memories of what happened to me start coming back. Once again, I turned to the very thing that was my crutch: food. But, this time I didn't allow the food to stay in my body I started purging often. This became a daily thing for me.

"I refuse to allow the weight to overtake me again", so I thought. Bulimia would become a part of my life for years. I got into a bad relationship, became stressed and my weight went out of control again. The only way I knew how to cope with the pain I was dealing with was with food.

Food had always been my way of dealing with things with everything I had been through in my life. Once I got out of the relationship I realized how much I had allowed my weight to get out of control. Now I needed to be free of the weight and all the pain I had endured. I turned to the one thing I knew that could help me: bulimia.

I knew I had to get this weight off me. I asked my best friend, "Why didn't you tell me I was this big?" She said, "you are so pretty friend, and you look good". For me I didn't feel pretty and, I was so disappointed with myself. I started purging on a daily basis. I was going through so much and I didn't know how to handle all the pain I kept enduring.

All I wanted was a way out. How did I fall into this trap? Searching for a way out from all the hurt. The way I'm coping I know it isn't healthy for me. I didn't know where to turn or who could help me handle everything I was going through.

Yes, I prayed plenty of times, but for me, the food was one of my soothing treatments. It couldn't take away what I was feeling, but I wanted it to. So many people will tell you how to handle your pain, but they've never endured what you have been through.

I tried to stop several times.

I was really in a depressed state and no one knew it, not even me. I was dealing with so much and I needed a way out. I'd hidden my pain behind food for so long while pretending to be in a happy place. Things were starting to get out of control.

Now, after purging so much I started popping blood vessels in my eyes. It got so bad I had to go to the doctor. Of course I didn't tell him exactly what had happened. My best friend, the only person in the loop of this traumatic secret, said if the doctor knew what really happened, he would have sent me to talk to someone.

I'm walking around now with a big red dot in my right eye and red lines in both eyes. I wasn't really telling people what happened to me because I wanted to keep it a secret. Not ready to face everything I was going through and there was too much that was going on in my head. To be honest I was ready to give up.

I had no choice but to stop purging until my eyes healed up. Trying to be careful of what I ate, because I didn't want to gain any more weight. The struggle was real. I was in a dark place trying to find a way out, not wanting to live anymore. The one thing I found comfort in, I could no longer indulge in for a while.

As I sit here, I realize this had become an addiction for me. Food was my addiction for many years. Guys would always tell me you are pretty for a thick girl. That used to bother me so much. Even though I had gotten my weight down it still wasn't where I wanted it to be.

I wasn't happy with who I was as this woman who has experienced so much pain and not understanding why. How do I keep on going with my life? Every time I looked in the mirror I hated how I looked. No matter how many compliments I may have gotten, I was never truly happy with who I was. All of the trauma I had endured I finally felt like I was hitting rock bottom and I didn't know how to escape it all.

As I started to get help with all the pain I was enduring, I still hid the part about me dealing with bulimia. I wasn't ready to face that part yet. I had to get past all of the hurt before I could even deal with my eating disorder. My wounds were so deep I was in for the fight of my life.

Suicide, depression, and bulimia had a stronghold over my life for years. I went to work every day not wanting to be there. I hated to get out of bed and I didn't even like my job anymore. I just wanted to be free of all this hurt.

Even though I was getting help with my pain, I was still in a dark place. I had to learn how to work through everything I was dealing with so I could get to the healing part. It took years to get to the healing part because I had been through so much. Learning how to take control of my life wasn't easy for me.

I had to realize I could no longer allow those things to keep me in bondage. Once I reached my healing from the past hurts I started to be in a better place. I was still dealing with bulimia - an addiction I couldn't shake yet. Even when I thought I had it under control, I would find myself overindulging in food until I would purge.

Let's be honest: We all have things about ourselves that we may not like, but we have learned how to live with the things we can't change.

I was learning how to love this person that had endured so much. I was this woman who wasn't skinny, and who wasn't in the 120-pound club. Some men who found me attractive and liked me wouldn't talk to me because of my weight.

My weight has been a factor for me since I was a little girl. With some of my friends I was always the plus size woman in the group. I knew I always had to bring "it". I had to make sure I was well kept at all

times, even when I was struggling on the inside. I still wasn't at the place where I loved how I looked.

People can tell you how beautiful you are all day, but you have to believe it yourself. I wasn't there yet and if I hadn't been afraid of surgery I probably would have had liposuction or gastric bypass. For me surgery wasn't an option. I had to conquer this weight another way. I know some of you are probably saying all you had to do was stop eating so much.

I would hear so called friends talk about my weight because I was no longer the small person I once was before. That would push me even more to be this small person again. But honestly, there was a war going on inside my head trying to please everyone but myself but I didn't know how to. When so much has been taken from you the majority of your life you push to please everyone.

How do I get to the place where I put me first, my life, my

weight, and even a peace of mind?

Well, I'm 45 years old now and I just realized that all this time I was trying to rescue the little girl I once was trying to be before all the hurt. I wanted to be that happy little girl again. I know now that I finally have the power over bulimia. Realizing that surviving everything I have been through, I conquered it all.

Dealing with bulimia hasn't been easy. This journey I have been on has had its ups and downs for me. At times I didn't know where to turn. I know I'm not the only woman that has or is dealing with bulimia. We hide our issues because of fear of what others might have to say about us, or not knowing how to deal with them.

Although, I can honestly say I still am dealing with weight issues, I am over bulimia. When I say I'm truly learning how to love me and put me first, I mean it! If I feel like I'm getting stressed I try to find other ways to handle it now instead of food. I have to break the cycle of things I use to do for comfort.

I know over the years I have suffered issues from dealing with bulimia. We don't realize the damage we can do to our bodies through our addictions. I just pray I haven't caused any permanent damage. I made a promise to myself to love me totally, with flaws and all. Now I'm learning how to put my life back together piece by piece.

No matter what we may endure in life we must find the strength to keep going. Everyday we are given a second chance at life. I plan on living each day to the best of my ability, not taking anything or anyone for granted. I now know that my life matters.

When you can finally realize what has kept you in bondage for so long it is truly a great feeling. I know I can never go back and be the little girl I once was, but I can learn how to love the woman I am today.

Overcoming bulimia has shown me I can conquer anything. The little girl I once was just wanted to be free from all the hurt and pain. She just wanted me to find the strength from within to keep going and overcome everything that was trying to take me out. I pray that everyone who is reading this and dealing with any hurt, or addiction find a way out and find complete healing.

I am on the road to complete healing of everything that once had control over my life. I'm striving to be a better me every day. It's a daily process, but I won't be defeated. I refuse to fall back into the things that kept me down.

Please whatever you do, don't give up. Keep fighting. There is purpose on the inside of you and no matter what you face you can't allow it to overtake you. You are a champion, an overcomer! With everything you have endured, it didn't take you out. Whatever you may be faced with right now just know you have the power to overcome it.

My journey hasn't been easy, but thank God I made it. Even when I wanted to give up God always sent someone to encourage me to keep going. Even when I was dealing with bulimia sometimes I wished I would die from it. But, God knew he had a plan for my life and death wasn't it.

I can finally breathe now. What had me held captive for 42 years no longer has power over me; therefore, I am finally free from it all. As I look in the mirror everyday, I now love the woman that I am becoming. When people didn't understand me or what I was going through, I had to push to keep going. I am so grateful to God for not giving up on me. He gave me another chance.

YOUR TAKE AWAYS FROM THIS CHAPTER

About the Authors

SHIRLEY D. LATOUR
Visionary Author

SHIRLEY D LATOUR is a native of Ft Wayne, IN currently residing in Killeen, TX. Retired Army Nurse Corps Veteran, she is a Transformational Speaker, International Best Selling Author and Minister of the Gospel. She is the CEO of SL Elite Publishing, a Christian Publishing Company, which she began in February 2019 with the launch of her first anthology *Grace To Recover*. Both previous books have become Amazon Best Sellers.

She is a radio personality on KRGN FM (download it on your cell phone from ANYWHERE in the world), Prison Break: Breaking down Walls Mind, Body and Spirit! She is also the Founder of Out Of The Shadows Outreach Ministry (non-profit), Founder and CEO of A Heart Pounding Success CPR Mobile business and runs her small business endeavors, to include health and wellness, through Shirley LaTour Enterprises, LLC.

Her passion is helping women realize their full potential, through Christ alone. She started having "Coming Out of The Shadows" events August 2016 and later officially founded "Out of The Shadows Outreach Ministry" (O.O.T.S) June 2017. She is a former First Lady, having made it through a 16 year broken "Christian" marriage and divorce and she wants to let others know that divorce is NOT the end of the world but an opportunity for NEW LIFE, a SECOND CHANCE! She has two wonderful children.

She is an avid volunteer in the surrounding communities and seeks to expand her reach around the world! With God, ALL things are possible. "To God Be the Glory!" slelitepublishing.com or support@slelitepublishing.com to inquire about becoming an author, co-author or shirleylatourenterprises.com for any of her services to the community.

Book her for speaking shirley@shirleylatourenterprises.com

DEMETRIUS GORDON Since 2009, Demetrius has been a noteworthy leader in the San Antonio area. You may know her from her work as the owner of Jamaica Jamaica Cuisine. She is not only a 22-year service veteran of the United States Army, but she is a veteran in the kitchen. From cooking quiches at 9, starting cooking clubs with friends, to teaming up with Jamaican husband to create Jamaica Jamaica Cuisine, Demetrius has shown a dedication to cooking and service. This service has extended to the community.

Known for helping, educating, and supporting young girls through Help Raise 1 Help Save 1 and women through various local organizations, Demetrius can often be found in the community feeding and assisting the homeless, returning citizens, veterans, the mature and teenagers. Often times, Jamaica Jamaica Cuisine is known to open their space and donate their time to the community and various programs such as Financial Literacy geared toward the youth, and Soul's Expressions, a showcase for the young artists, along with various community and national relief efforts.

Demetrius is setting a new standard for how to care for

your community. Her commitment to developing our youth into productive members of society is changing the way the community views the young, homeless and more. She loves helping people. She has spent the majority of her life gaining experience in leadership, marketing and service. Although her primary day-to-day functions also include being a devoted mother and wife, she also enjoys making the forgotten members of the community thrive.

deme.gordon@gmail.com

YVONNE TIJERINA A Daughter, Sister, Friend, Wife and Mother, author Yvonne Tijerina justly and passionately believes in the CREATOR, Love, Faith, Peace, Honor and Respect. For all life and the multitude of unique qualities throughout our world that give us our splendor. She is a fervent advocate not just for her daughter but also for others on the Autism spectrum or diagnosed with physical or intellectual differences. With the support of her family; as an entrepreneur she is indomitable in establishing sustainable generational wealth. "The CREATOR and your Why are bigger than fear!" – Yvonne Tijerina

August Sisters Homespun Emporium LLC aka ASH-Emporium online at ASHEmporiumET.com

TORRI EUGENE is a wife, mother, sister, daughter but most of all, Author Torri Eugene is a SURVIVOR. Raised in the hostile streets of Harlem, NY, she had to quickly learn how to get by. At the age of 14 she was diagnosed with bipolar disorder, ADHD, and anxiety disorder; all the while being placed in the foster care system. She had to learn how to live day to day with some life skills that were obtained in therapy. Some were obtained just by going through everyday struggles. Later in life she would get the opportunity to see the healing power of God work throughout her life.

She had her share of tribulations: chronic homelessness, molestation, suicide attempts…and that's just to name a few. However, by the grace of God and the help of therapy she has overcome them all. Today she is happily married, a member of the Black Women In Business (BWIB) Killeen chapter, an independent lifestyle consultant for Bedroom Kandi and that's just the beginning. She is now obtaining her associates degree in communication and media technology.

Visit her at www.bedroomkandi.com/10654

MONICA WASHINGTON is originally from Waco Texas but calls Harker Heights her home, which she shares with two amazing children and her loving spouse. She always had a passion for helping others. Since opening her heart to the love of Jesus she has volunteered at various events from Mothers Against Drunk Driving to nursing homes and even pre-k classrooms at Harker Heights Elementary.

Early 2019 Monica had a revelation about the homeless in central Texas, which led her to become the founder of Operation Faith. A program she started on her own that passes out food and personal items to the areas homeless. She is currently working on her debut book Broken Grace: The Rare Diamond with the hoping reaching many lives she does what she does best; inspire and help others.

WANDA "SISTAH SOLDIER" PETTY, is an inspirational speaker, a God-fearing creative thinker, and a serial entrepreneur. The creator of SHE VET™ iNC. Media Productions, the Founder of The National Resource Society for Women Veterans, Inc. (where she assumes the role as Host and Visionary Producer of SHE VET™ iNSPIRES television show), and the Master Trainer / Recruiter of SHE WORKS Digital (providing IT Project Management recruitment and virtual training).

Her background consists of being a Human Resource Manager/Trainer and Recruiter. She retired with 21 years of active duty service in the Army and is passionate about helping women, service members, and veterans deplete barriers that attempt to stunt their personal and professional development.

She's a spirit warrior teacher, transformational leader, high impact trainer, and the co-author of Amazon Bestsellers "Behind the Rank, Vol 2, a published author of "A Spirit Warrior's Mindset™; Life Mastery Series" and "The Art in Me™; Unleash

Your Uniqueness Through the Power of Creativity". As a spirit warrior, she's committed to eradicating unemployment and creat-

ing diversity in the working world. She strategically teaches others how to become masterfully indispensable in their career using their spiritual gifts to build divine relationships and generate a future with possibilities.

www.sistahsoldier.com

info@sistahsoldier.com

Photo Credit: Yukiko Avila Photography

HEIDI R. LOPEZ is an Army veteran who obtained several years of medical training and experience during her time in service. She was honorably discharged and continues her dedication to service as a Civil Service employee with 19 years and 11 months of service.

She continued her schooling post-military and in 2010 she obtained her BS in Multidisciplinary studies from Grantham University. Her future plans include obtaining her Master's degree as well.

Heidi currently holds a Notary Public license for the State of California and she's also an Independent Consultant for Paparazzi Accessories.

Heidi is from the "City of Angels", Los Angeles, California and is a single mother to a wonderful teenager, Joshua. Heidi, along with her son, is very involved in church ministries at their home church.

They also volunteer with local organizations that focus on helping homeless individuals and she strives to teach her son about selfless service and sharing God's love to the less fortunate.

HEIDIRTUGMON@YAHOO.COM

www.bosschickbling.com

DORLEAN WASHINGTON is a Sister in Christ who loves Jesus. She is eternally grateful that she has overcome deeply rooted conditions through deliverance and healing; and has been granted the opportunity to help others.

Ms. Washington raised three children and is now a grandmother and great grandmother. She has served as a professional businesswoman for over 30 years and has traveled throughout the United States, Europe, Israel and Africa.

Ms. Dee has established DeeOnyx Divine Ministries, LLC. Which entails professional life changing businesses such as: Resurrection Life Counseling Service, DeeOnyx Mobile Notary, DeeOnyx Books, Legal Shield, and Mary Kay Skin Care Beauty Consultant. She serves in her Church as well as in the community as a KCOP (Killeen Civilian on Patrol).

Dorlean pursued higher education in Ministry and has acquired an Associate degree in Biblical Studies, A Master's degree in Faith Based Counseling, and a Doctorate Degree in Pastoral Counseling. Dr. Dee is a

licensed minister who has a passion to see souls saved that

they may have freedom from rooted bondages in order to establish their true purpose in Christ.

dorlean.washington@yahoo.com

254-338-2778

MICHELE GRAHAM, RN, BSN, a migrant from The Ivory Coast (West Africa) now residing in Texas, is what you would call a BOSS LADY. She is a business mogul, heading several businesses simultaneously while furthering her education.

Michele is a Registered Nurse and soon to become a Family Nurse Practitioner, after just two more semesters, anticipating graduation in 2020. She is the owner of Owner-operator at Point of Grace Home Health Agency, Sublime Body Health and Wellness Spa, and Aubrel Travel Agency, all while serving veterans as an RN at the VA Hospital. Now she can add Author to her resume!

She desires to serve our country by giving back to our veteran population. She is a mother of three children: a son and two daughters.

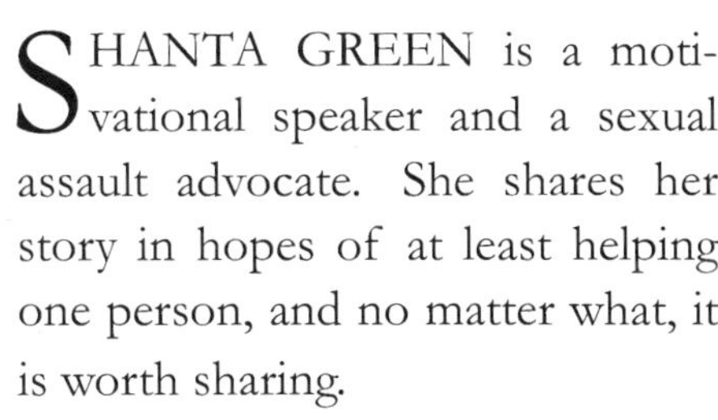

S HANTA GREEN is a moti-vational speaker and a sexual assault advocate. She shares her story in hopes of at least helping one person, and no matter what, it is worth sharing.

Her goal is to reach as many people as possible who are dealing with things they haven't yet healed from or they are too afraid to speak out. I am your voice. Shanta has started her own website justasktay.com and also has a Facebook page called Just Ask Tay. She shares her life with you about things she has endured in her life and has healed from.

About Out of The Shadows Outreach Ministry (O.O.T.S.)

Out Of the Shadows (formerly named Coming Out of The Shadows) was first given to Shirley LaTour, Founder, as an assignment for healing. After the first event was held on August 13, 2016, she quickly realized that this was NOT just for her but discovered that many women need to "Come Out of The Shadows". This is a GOD ASSIGNMENT.

Women struggle inwardly with many things. We hold up as champs on the outside but many are broken on the inside. There is so much to be said of women. Let us be VICTORIOUS, overcomers and women of faith who UNAPOLOGETICALLY walk out the assignment of God for our lives; whether at home as a wife and or mother, on the job, in business, or in ministry. Time for healing for women all over the world, starting right in Killeen, TX! WALK IT OUT!

The very thing God prompted Shirley to do two (2) years before divorce, helping other women break free of fear and everything holding them back from their God given purpose, broke her free! She is a firm believer that God can and will do the impossible in every area of life for those that truly believe His Word. The WORD HEALS, NOT time. No more shall we live in the shadows!

Officially founded as a Non-Profit Organization June 2017, O.O.T.S. endeavors to minister to the needs of women everywhere, bringing hope for a brighter tomorrow.

The ministry serves women who have been held back from being their true selves and all they were predestined to do in this life, those searching for a better way of living, breaking free of self-doubt, hatred, fear and so much more that hinders our walk with Christ and others.

Next stop: Reaching men! We all have a purpose, sometimes hidden: buried under past hurt and pain.

O.O.T.S also aims to give scholarships to children of Single parent homes and foster children phasing out of the system. Consider being a blessing to those in need.

O.O.T.S. is held quarterly in Killeen, weekly meet-ups, movies and study sessions are on various topics of interest to women. Follow OOTS on FB and on our website!

FB: www.facebook.com/OOTShadows

Website: www.ootshadow.org

How YOU can be involved

Shirley would love to hear your feedback on this book on Amazon, on Facebook and/or by email support@slelite-publishing.com! Please know that by providing feedback you are helping us do better in reaching the world. Your comments will be expressed on our website.

You may remain anonymous if you wish, just state so and we will honor your request!

MEN

Still here men? If you are interested in being an author by writing a chapter of your story as an uplift to other men or writing your very own book, reach out to us at support@slelitepublishing.com with your inquiry.

The first of its kind is projected for release January 17, 2020. Even if you have never written a word on paper before of your story, we can and will coach you through the process.

MARRIED COUPLES

Been on the brink of divorce before and now THRIV-ING in your marriage (to the same person) with the help of the Lord? We want to hear about it! Send in your inquiry to support@slelitepublishing.com.